SAVEUR
SOUPS
AND STEWS

THE EDITORS OF SAVEUR

TABLE OF CONTENTS

INTRODUCTION

There are, admittedly, a couple of things that can make us as happy as a great bowl of soup makes us. The love of a child? Sure. World peace? That sounds nice. But let's be honest: That stuff is tricky and time-consuming. And frankly, it is not nearly as dependable as the easy, economical alchemy—let's call it magic—of transforming a pile of roasted bones and cut-up vegetables into a steaming stockpot of comfort that will nourish you for a week. Hot or cold, rigorously simple or riotously complex, soups and stews are the endlessly adaptable answers to the riddle of life's bounty and the nagging question of what to cook on a Tuesday night with a can of beans and some kale wilting in the fridge.

SAVEUR celebrates the cuisines of the world, and as the sheer variety here attests—from Thai shrimp curry to an all-American chicken and white bean chili—things stewing in pots are a global concern. They might not bring peace in our time, but surely there's nothing as universal or as unifying as the desire for a bowl of something stabilizing, with a drizzle of olive oil or a dollop of yogurt on top and some bread on the side for dipping.

Adam

ADAM SACHS
SAVEUR EDITOR-IN-CHIEF

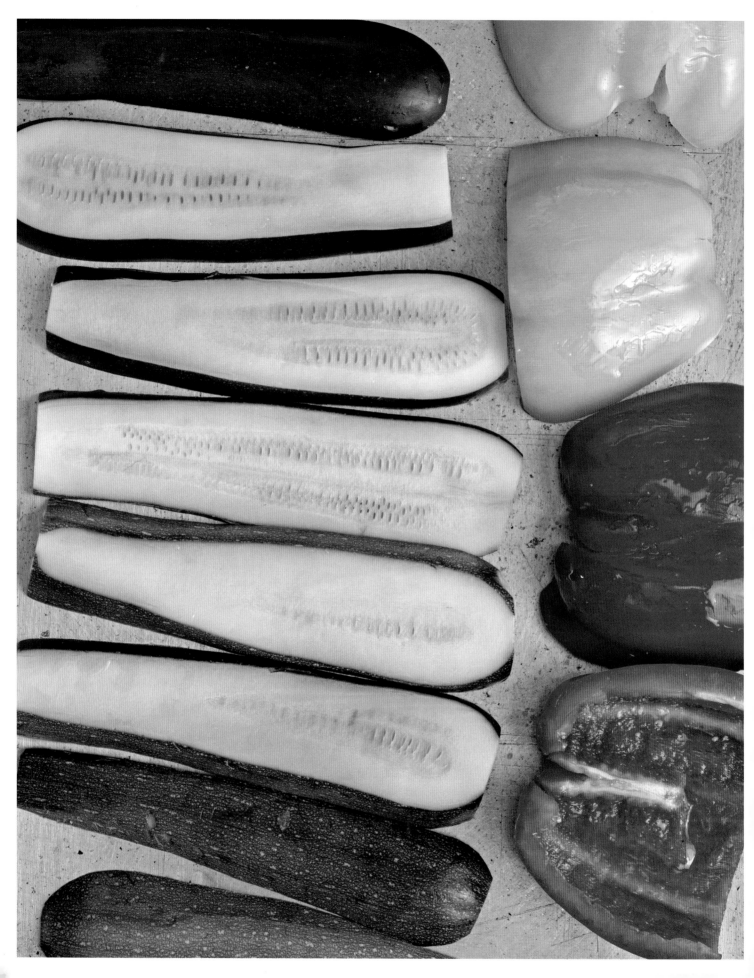

MEAT

For this traditional Jewish-Iraqi dish, lamb meatballs, lightly sweetened with currants, are braised in a brilliantly hued, tangy beet stew, which is served atop pale gold basmati rice.

BEET STEW WITH LAMB MEATBALLS

FOR THE MEATBALLS

- 1 tbsp. extra-virgin olive oil
- 1 small yellow onion, finely chopped
- ½ lb. ground lamb
- 2 tbsp. dried currants
- 1½ tbsp. coarsely chopped fresh flat-leaf parsley
- 1 tbsp. pine nuts
- ½ tsp. paprika
- 1 egg, lightly beaten
  Kosher salt and freshly ground black pepper, to taste

FOR THE RICE

- 1½ cups basmati rice, soaked in water for 20 minutes and drained
- 2 tsp. kosher salt
- 1 tsp. turmeric

FOR THE STEW

- 6 small red beets (about 1 lb.), peeled and cut into sixths
- 5 tbsp. extra-virgin olive oil
- 1½ tsp. curry powder
- 1½ tsp. ground coriander
- 1½ tsp. ground cumin
- 1 tsp. turmeric
- ¾ tsp. paprika
- ½ tsp. ground ginger
- ⅛ tsp. cayenne pepper

- 3 cloves garlic, mashed into a paste
- 1 medium yellow onion, finely chopped
- ¼ cup tomato paste
- 6 tbsp. fresh lemon juice
- 2 tbsp. sugar
  Kosher salt and freshly ground black pepper, to taste
- 1 tbsp. finely chopped fresh flat-leaf parsley, to garnish
- 1 tbsp. pine nuts, to garnish

SERVES 4–6

1 Make the meatballs: Heat oil in a 10″ skillet over medium-high. Add onion and cook, stirring occasionally, until slightly caramelized, about 7 minutes. Transfer onion to a bowl and let cool slightly. Add remaining meatball ingredients to the bowl and mix until combined. Using wet hands, roll mixture into twelve 1½″ balls and transfer to a parchment paper–lined baking sheet. Cover with plastic wrap and chill for 30 minutes.

2 Make the rice: Combine rice, salt, turmeric, and 2 cups water in a 2-qt. saucepan and bring to a boil. Reduce heat to low and cook, covered, for 10 minutes. Remove rice from heat and fluff with a fork. Keep warm.

3 Make the stew: Combine beets and 6 cups water in a 4-qt. saucepan and bring to a boil. Reduce heat to medium-low and cook, covered, until beets are tender, about 30 minutes. Using a slotted spoon, transfer beets to a bowl; reserve cooking liquid.

4 Mix 3 tbsp. oil, the curry powder, coriander, cumin, turmeric, paprika, ginger, cayenne, and garlic paste in a bowl and set aside. Heat remaining oil in a 6-qt. saucepan over medium-high. Add onion and cook, stirring occasionally, until golden, about 7 minutes. Add reserved spice paste and tomato paste and cook, stirring constantly, until mixture is slightly caramelized, about 3 minutes. Stir in reserved beet cooking liquid, the lemon juice, sugar, salt, and pepper and simmer for 5 minutes. Add meatballs and cook, stirring occasionally and gently, until meatballs are cooked through, about 8 minutes. If necessary, skim surface of stew. Add reserved beets and cook until warmed through, 1–2 minutes more. Spoon rice into bowls and top with stew. Garnish with parsley and pine nuts.

Many Texans don't like beans in their chili. So while they might not approve of this robust Kansas City–style variation, the tender pork shoulder, rich depth of flavor, and ample heat make it irresistible.

KANSAS CITY–STYLE CHILI

1   lb. boneless pork shoulder, trimmed

Kosher salt and freshly ground black pepper, to taste

⅓   cup packed light brown sugar

2   tsp. garlic powder

1   tsp. ground cumin

2   12-oz. bottles pale ale–style beer

6   oz. sliced bacon, finely chopped

10 cloves garlic, finely chopped

1   jalapeño chile, stemmed, seeded, and finely chopped

1   large red bell pepper, stemmed, seeded, and finely chopped

1   large sweet onion, such as Vidalia, finely chopped

¼   cup tomato paste

3   tbsp. dark red chile powder

½   tbsp. Aleppo pepper

1   tsp. crushed red chile flakes

2   bay leaves

2   cups chicken stock

2   28-oz. cans whole peeled tomatoes, crushed by hand

2   15.5-oz. cans dark red kidney beans, drained and rinsed

2   tbsp. hot sauce

2   tbsp. Worcestershire sauce

Shredded cheddar, to garnish

Sliced scallions and finely chopped red onion, to garnish

Cornbread, for serving (optional)

1 Heat oven to 500°F. Place pork in a 9″ x 13″ baking dish and season with salt and pepper. Mix brown sugar, garlic powder, and cumin in a bowl; rub sugar mixture all over pork. Roast until browned, 30–35 minutes. Reduce heat to 300°F. Add 1 bottle of beer and cover baking dish tightly with aluminum foil; roast until pork is very tender, about 2 hours. Let pork rest for 20 minutes, then shred into bite-size pieces.

2 Heat bacon in an 8-qt. saucepan over medium-high. Cook until fat is rendered and bacon is crisp, 5–7 minutes. Add garlic, jalapeño, bell pepper, and onion and cook until soft, 10–12 minutes. Add tomato paste, chile powder, Aleppo pepper, chile flakes, and bay leaves and cook until lightly caramelized, about 2 minutes. Add remaining bottle of beer, the stock, tomatoes, and beans and bring to a boil. Reduce heat to medium-low and cook, partially covered, until chili is thickened, 1½–2 hours. Stir in reserved shredded pork, the hot sauce, and Worcestershire. Ladle chili into bowls, garnish with cheddar, scallions, and red onion and crumble cornbread over the top.

SERVES 8–10

THE HISTORY OF CHILI

There are as many stories about where chili came from as there are ways to make it, but they all begin in or around what today is Texas. The word itself came into English by way of the Spaniards, who in turn got it from Nahuatl, an Aztec language. *Chili* referred to peppers, which Native Americans had cultivated for millennia. The Spanish arrived with cattle, and somewhere along the way, cuisines blended and a hungry soul looking for a bowl of something wonderful thought to mix handfuls of peppers with ground beef, and *chili con carne* was born.

No sooner had the first "bowl of red" been ladled than people began to dispute what made an authentic chili. Beans or no beans? Is it still chili if the meat is venison? So began a thousand disputes, and the proliferation of local variations.

Early on, chili was dried, salted, pressed into bricks, and carted on long journeys through the inhospitable Southwestern frontier: Drop a brick into boiling water and, presto, dinner was served. By the late 19th century, enterprising cooks were commercializing chili, traveling far to set up shop at the Columbian Exposition in Chicago, where visitors could buy a bowl at the San Antonio Chili Stand. The 20th century saw the dish canned, extending its availability and simplifying its serving. In the 1960s, President Lyndon B. Johnson's appetite for his wife's Pedernales River Chili made the dish so famous that the White House had recipe cards printed. Look for the recipe at Johnson's presidential library in Austin or on the library's website.

This beef and root vegetable stew is made with armagnac, chocolate, and, traditionally, madiran wine, a rich, concentrated, and highly tannic wine produced in Gascony, in southwestern France. If you can't find it, pinot noir is a good alternative and makes a lighter, more nuanced broth.

GASCON-STYLE BEEF STEW

3 oz. slab bacon, cut into ½″ matchsticks

3½ lb. beef chuck, trimmed and cut into 2″ pieces

Kosher salt and freshly ground black pepper, to taste

10 cloves garlic, coarsely chopped

3 medium carrots, cut into ½″ pieces

2 parsnips, peeled and cut into ½″ pieces

1 large yellow onion, cut into ½″ pieces

⅓ cup armagnac or other brandy

2 cups beef stock

1 750-ml. bottle madiran wine or a light-bodied red wine, such as pinot noir

3 sprigs fresh flat-leaf parsley

3 sprigs fresh thyme

2 bay leaves

2 sprigs fresh rosemary

2 oz. unsweetened dark chocolate, coarsely chopped

3 tbsp. unsalted butter

4 oz. porcini or white button mushrooms, trimmed and quartered

Country bread, for serving (optional)

SERVES 6-8

1 Heat bacon in an 8-qt. saucepan over medium-high. Cook, stirring occasionally, until fat is rendered and bacon is crisp, 5–7 minutes. Using a slotted spoon, transfer bacon to paper towels to drain and set aside. Season beef with salt and pepper. Working in batches, cook, turning as needed, until browned, 12–14 minutes. Transfer beef to a bowl and set aside. Add garlic, carrots, parsnips, and onion to the pan and cook, stirring occasionally, until slightly caramelized, 10–12 minutes. Add armagnac; deglaze, stirring and scraping up browned bits from bottom of pan, and cook until reduced by half, 1–2 minutes. Add stock, wine, salt, and pepper and bring to a boil. Place parsley, thyme, bay leaves, and rosemary on a piece of cheesecloth; tie into a tight bundle and add to pan. Return beef to pan and reduce heat to medium-low; cook, partially covered, until beef is very tender, 2–2½ hours. Uncover and stir in reserved bacon, the chocolate, salt, and pepper and cook until chocolate is melted, about 5 minutes more. Keep stew warm.

2 Melt butter in a 12″ skillet over medium-high. Add mushrooms and cook, stirring occasionally, until golden brown, 4–6 minutes. Season with salt and pepper, and transfer to stew. Discard herb bundle and ladle stew into bowls. Serve with bread on the side.

THE ART OF THE BOUQUET GARNI

A bouquet garni is a little bundle of herbs that makes all the difference when you're cooking soups and stews. It infuses them with aromatic layers of flavor, enhancing the other ingredients by lending a subtle herbal base note.

Making a bouquet garni requires only a few sprigs of fresh or dried herbs, some string, and sometimes a piece of cheesecloth. The classic French combination calls for 3 sprigs each fresh flat-leaf parsley and thyme and 2 bay leaves tied together and placed in the pot to perfume the liquid. Depending on the ingredients in the soup or stew, you can add other herbs and aromatics to suit your taste. Tarragon and thyme work well with seafood, and rosemary and oregano are wonderful with meat-based soups. When using ingredients like garlic cloves or peppercorns in your bouquet garni, bundle them together in a cheesecloth pouch, and don't forget to remove the pouch from the pot before serving.

The big flavor in this Tunisian stew comes from beef short ribs that are cooked until meltingly tender and well-seasoned beef meatballs. Just before the stew is served, chopped spinach and cooked white beans are added to the pot and simmered until heated through.

TUNISIAN SHORT RIB & MEATBALL STEW

FOR THE MEATBALLS

2	tbsp. extra-virgin olive oil
1	small yellow onion, finely chopped
1	lb. ground chuck
1	tbsp. freshly ground black pepper
1	tbsp. ground cumin
1	tbsp. finely chopped fresh cilantro
1	tbsp. finely chopped fresh flat-leaf parsley
2¼	tsp. kosher salt
1½	tsp. paprika
¾	tsp. ground cinnamon
1	egg, lightly beaten

FOR THE STEW

¼	cup extra-virgin olive oil
1	lb. flanken-cut beef short ribs
	Kosher salt and freshly ground black pepper, to taste
4	cloves garlic, finely chopped
1	large yellow onion, finely chopped
5	cups beef stock
6	oz. spinach leaves, coarsely chopped
1	15-oz. can white beans, such as navy or cannellini, drained and rinsed

SERVES 6–8

1 Make the meatballs: Heat oil in a 6-qt. saucepan over medium-high. Add onion and cook, stirring occasionally, until soft, about 5 minutes. Using a slotted spoon, transfer onion to a large bowl; reserve saucepan. Add ground chuck, pepper, cumin, cilantro, parsley, salt, paprika, cinnamon, and egg to the bowl and mix until combined. Using wet hands, roll mixture into about 40 balls. Return saucepan to medium-high. Working in batches, cook meatballs, turning as needed, until browned, 4–6 minutes. Transfer meatballs to a plate and cover with plastic wrap; set aside.

2 Make the stew: Return saucepan to medium-high and add oil. Season short ribs with salt and pepper. Working in batches, cook, flipping once, until browned, about 8 minutes. Transfer short ribs to a plate and set aside. Add garlic and onion to pan and cook, stirring, until lightly caramelized, 5–7 minutes. Return ribs to pan and add stock; bring to a boil. Reduce heat to medium-low and cook, covered, until short ribs are tender, about 1 hour. Add reserved meatballs and cook until tender, about 8 minutes. Add spinach and beans and cook until spinach is wilted and beans are warmed through, about 4 minutes more. To serve, divide meatballs between bowls and ladle stew over the top.

To get through bitterly cold winters, Russian cooks rely on this thick mix of five types of fresh and cured beef and pork. The bounty of meat gives the soup heft, while the combination of pickles, capers, and olives delivers a welcome saltiness and tang.

RUSSIAN SWEET & SOUR BEEF SOUP

1	lb. beef chuck, trimmed
1/2	lb. kielbasa sausage
4	oz. boneless ham steak
2	oz. hard salami
4	whole black peppercorns
3	whole allspice berries
1	bay leaf
4	oz. sliced bacon, finely chopped
1	large yellow onion, thinly sliced
1	rib celery, thinly sliced
1/4	small head green cabbage, cored and thinly shredded
	Kosher salt and freshly ground black pepper, to taste
6	tbsp. tomato paste
1	15-oz. can whole peeled tomatoes, crushed by hand
5	cups beef stock
1 1/2	large dill pickles, coarsely chopped
1 1/2	tbsp. capers, drained
1/4	cup pitted black olives, thinly sliced
1 1/2	tbsp. sugar
1/2	lemon, thinly sliced and seeded
	Coarsely chopped fresh flat-leaf parsley, sliced scallions, and sour cream, to garnish

SERVES 8

1 Cut beef, kielbasa, ham, and salami into ¼″ pieces and set aside. Place peppercorns, allspice, and bay leaf on a piece of cheesecloth; tie into a tight bundle and set aside.

2 Heat bacon over medium-high in a 6-qt. saucepan. Cook until fat is rendered and bacon is crisp, 5–7 minutes. Using a slotted spoon, transfer bacon to a bowl and set aside. Add beef, kielbasa, ham, and salami to pan and cook until browned, 6–8 minutes. Add onion, celery, cabbage, salt, and pepper and cook until soft, 4–6 minutes. Stir in tomato paste and cook, stirring occasionally, until slightly caramelized, about 2 minutes. Return bacon to pot and add spice bundle. Add tomatoes and stock and bring to a boil. Reduce heat to medium and add pickles and capers. Cook, stirring occasionally, until beef is tender, 40–45 minutes.

3 Remove spice bundle. Stir in olives, sugar, lemon, salt, and pepper. Ladle soup into bowls and garnish with parsley, scallions, and sour cream.

HOW TO CORRECT OVERSALTING

We've all been there. You spend the day sweating over a hot stove, only to realize too late: You've over-salted the soup. Don't freak out—or throw the soup out. There are ways to salvage your labor. Some people peel and quarter a potato, add it to the pot, and then let the dish simmer for 15 minutes. The potato will absorb some of the saltiness; just be sure to discard it before serving. Another good trick is to add a bit of sour cream, brown sugar, vinegar, or lemon juice to help balance out the salt. You can also purée some cooked white rice with water and add that to the soup or stew, or you can add extra vegetables and grains to absorb some of the salt.

Adobo is the national dish of the Philippines: pork, chicken, or both braised in seasoned vinegar with garlic, bay, and soy sauce. Regional variations abound, but no matter how it's made, adobo always delivers a distinctive piquant flavor and aroma thanks to the presence of palm vinegar, soy sauce, and fish sauce.

PHILIPPINE PORK STEW

2½ lb. boneless pork shoulder, trimmed and cut into 2″ pieces

½ cup palm vinegar

3 tbsp. soy sauce

1 tsp. whole black peppercorns, crushed

12 cloves garlic, crushed

1 bay leaf

2 tbsp. lard or canola oil

4 cups cooked white rice, for serving

Patis (Philippine fish sauce), for serving (optional)

SERVES 4

1 Combine pork, vinegar, soy sauce, peppercorns, garlic, and bay leaf in a large bowl. Cover and refrigerate for at least 8 hours or up to overnight.

2 Combine pork mixture and 2 cups water in a 6-qt. Dutch oven and bring to a boil, skimming any foam that rises to the surface. Reduce heat to medium-low and cook, covered, until pork is tender, about 1½ hours. Pour the pork stew into a colander set over a bowl; discard the bay leaf. Separate pork and garlic and set both aside. Return liquid to pot and bring to a simmer over medium. Cook until reduced to 1½ cups, about 25 minutes. Transfer stock to a bowl and set aside.

3 Add lard to the pot and melt over medium-high. Working in batches, cook reserved pork, turning as needed, until browned, about 10 minutes. Add reserved garlic and cook, stirring occasionally, until golden, about 2 minutes. Stir in reserved stock and reduce heat to medium-low; cook for 5 minutes more. To serve, divide rice between 4 bowls and ladle adobo over top. Drizzle with Patis.

This one-pot stew from the Baltic nation of Latvia features all three of the country's mealtime staples: pork, potatoes, and cabbage. They're ensconced in a delicious sweet-and-sour broth made from a simple yet surprising combination of tomato sauce and prunes.

LATVIAN PORK & CABBAGE STEW

3   tbsp. canola oil

1¾   lb. boneless pork shoulder, cut into 1½″ pieces

  Kosher salt and freshly ground black pepper, to taste

3   cloves garlic, finely chopped

1   large yellow onion, finely chopped

1   cup pitted prunes, halved

3   ribs celery, cut into ½″-thick slices

4   medium carrots, peeled and cut into ¾″-thick rounds

1   medium head cabbage, cored and coarsely shredded

3½   lb. Yukon gold potatoes, peeled and cut into 1½″ pieces

⅔   cup canned tomato sauce

1   tbsp. red wine vinegar

1   tbsp. sugar

  Sour cream, to garnish

SERVES 8–10

1 Heat oil in an 8-qt. Dutch oven over medium-high. Season pork with salt and pepper. Working in batches, cook pork, turning as needed, until browned, about 10 minutes. Using a slotted spoon, transfer pork to a bowl and set aside.

2 Add garlic and onion to pot and cook, stirring occasionally, until soft, about 4 minutes. Without stirring, return pork to pot in a single layer. In this order, add prunes, celery, carrots, cabbage, and potatoes in individual layers. Whisk tomato sauce, vinegar, sugar, and 1 cup water in a bowl and pour mixture over potatoes. Cover and cook, shaking pot occasionally but not stirring, until pork and vegetables are tender, about 1 hour. Ladle stew into bowls and garnish each serving with a dollop of sour cream.

This New Mexico staple celebrates the state's native chiles in a thick purée that glazes tender chunks of pork shoulder. Lightly pungent and earthy New Mexico chiles, in both dried and powder form, are available at many specialty markets.

NEW MEXICAN RED CHILE & PORK STEW

5 oz. dried New Mexico chiles, stemmed

8 cups boiling water

2 tbsp. honey

2 tbsp. New Mexico chile powder

1 tbsp. white wine vinegar

2 tsp. ground cumin

1½ tsp. ground cloves

⅛ tsp. cayenne pepper

Juice of ½ lime

5 tbsp. extra-virgin olive oil

3 lb. boneless pork shoulder, cut into 1½″ pieces

Kosher salt and freshly ground black pepper, to taste

Corn tortillas, warmed, for serving (optional)

SERVES 8–10

1 Heat chiles in a 6-qt. Dutch oven over medium-high. Cook, turning once, until toasted, about 5 minutes. Transfer chiles to a large bowl and add boiling water; let sit until softened, about 20 minutes. Drain chiles, reserving 1½ cups soaking liquid. Transfer chiles and reserved liquid to a blender. Add honey, chile powder, vinegar, cumin, cloves, cayenne, and lime juice and purée until smooth. Set sauce aside.

2 Return pot to medium-high and add oil. Season pork with salt and pepper. Working in batches, cook pork, turning as needed, until browned, about 12 minutes. Add reserved chile sauce and bring to a boil. Reduce heat to medium-low and cook, stirring occasionally, until sauce is thickened and pork is tender, about 1½ hours. Ladle stew into bowls and serve with tortillas.

Infused with smoky, mild-to-hot *guajillo* chiles, this hearty stew can be made with various tough cuts of beef, but oxtails are the most flavorful choice. Served with rice, the dish is a favorite meal across Mexico.

OXTAIL & GUAJILLO CHILE STEW

1½   lb. beef oxtails, trimmed and cut into 2″ lengths

Kosher salt and freshly ground black pepper, to taste

6   cloves garlic

1   small white onion, quartered

2   cups boiling water

4   dried guajillo chiles, stemmed and seeded

1   plum tomato, cored and quartered

2   tbsp. canola oil

1   lb. small Yukon gold potatoes, cut into wedges

1   tsp. dried oregano, preferably Mexican

Cooked white rice, for serving

Lime wedges, for serving

SERVES 8

1 Season oxtails with salt and pepper and place in a 6-qt. Dutch oven. Add 2 cloves garlic, 1 quarter of the onion, and 6 cups water and bring to a boil. Reduce heat to medium-low and cook, covered, until beef is tender, about 2 hours. Using tongs, transfer oxtails to a bowl and set aside. Pour cooking liquid through a fine-mesh sieve set over a bowl and discard solids. Set cooking liquid aside.

2 Meanwhile, combine the water and chiles in a blender and let sit until soft, about 30 minutes. Add remaining garlic and onion and the tomato; purée until smooth. Pour chile purée through a fine-mesh sieve into a bowl and set aside.

3 Heat oil in a 6-qt. saucepan over medium-high. Cook reserved chile purée, stirring constantly, until slightly reduced, about 8 minutes. Stir in reserved oxtails and their cooking liquid, potatoes, and oregano and bring to a boil. Reduce heat to medium-low and cook, stirring occasionally, until potatoes are tender, about 20 minutes. Season with salt and pepper. Ladle stew into bowls and serve with rice and lime wedges.

WORKING WITH CHILES

Sold both fresh and dried, chiles add heat, smokiness, and depth of flavor to soups and stews. Whether the chiles are used as a garnish, as a cooked or raw ingredient, or as a purée, here are some key tips on working with them.

HANDLING CHILES Wear gloves when working with hot chiles to avoid a painful burning sensation on your hands. As soon as you have finished working with the chiles, thoroughly wash your hands, cutting board, and knife with hot, soapy water.

REDUCING HEAT To decrease the heat in a fresh chile, lay it on a cutting board and, using a small, sharp knife, slit the chile lengthwise. Run the knife along the inside of the chile to remove the seeds and uppermost layer of textured flesh. Reserve the seeds for diners who want more heat.

ROASTING & PEELING FRESH CHILES Place fresh chiles directly under a preheated broiler or over a direct flame (on a grill or on the burner on a gas stove). Using tongs, turn the chiles until the skin is blistered and blackened on all sides, 10 to 15 minutes. Transfer the chiles to a paper bag and close loosely. When the chiles are cool, peel or rub away the charred skin.

TOASTING DRIED CHILES Heat a heavy frying pan or griddle over high. Place the dried chiles on the hot pan and, using tongs, turn them often until fragrant and lightly toasted.

SOAKING DRIED CHILES Rehydrate dried chiles by soaking them in boiling water to cover until softened, about 15 minutes. Use the soaked chiles and the soaking liquid in puréed sauces.

Caldo verde, a national favorite of Portugal, celebrates the country's classic pairing of cured pork with hearty vegetables. The "green soup" traditionally combines finely shredded kale with potato chunks and chorizo slices. This riff on that dish replaces the dark greens with Savoy cabbage and spices up the soup with chile flakes.

SPICY CABBAGE & CHORIZO SOUP

½ lb. chorizo, casing removed, sliced ¼" thick

2 tbsp. extra-virgin olive oil, plus more for drizzling

1 large yellow onion, coarsely chopped

4 cloves garlic, finely chopped

¼ tsp. crushed red chile flakes, plus more to taste

1 lb. Yukon gold potatoes, peeled and cut into 1" pieces

1 lb. Savoy or green cabbage, cored and thinly shredded

1 15-oz. can navy or Great Northern beans, drained and rinsed

Juice of ½ lemon

Kosher salt and freshly ground black pepper, to taste

1 Heat chorizo and oil in a 6-qt. saucepan over medium-high. Cook until fat from chorizo is rendered and chorizo is crisp, 3–4 minutes. Add onion and cook, stirring occasionally, until onion is soft, about 4 minutes. Add garlic and chile flakes and cook until fragrant, 1–2 minutes. Add potatoes and 8 cups water and bring to a boil. Reduce heat to medium and cook until potatoes are just tender, 12–15 minutes.

2 Stir in cabbage and beans and cook until cabbage is wilted, 5–10 minutes. Remove from heat and stir in lemon juice, salt, and pepper. Ladle soup into bowls, drizzle with oil, and serve.

SERVES 8

Thick and spicy chili con carne is a staple in the state of Texas, and there are as many versions of it there as there are cattle. But any purist will tell you that this revered dish should never contain beans or tomatoes. Slow-braised beef and pork shoulder melt into a sauce of fiery chiles with plenty of garlic, cumin, and oregano and the smoky undertone of bacon.

CHILI CON CARNE

6   large dried guajillo chiles

6   dried chiles de árbol

4   cups boiling water

2   tbsp. rendered bacon fat

1   lb. beef shoulder, cut into 1/4″ cubes

1   lb. pork shoulder, cut into 1/4″ cubes

5   cloves garlic, finely chopped

1   small yellow onion, finely chopped

1   tbsp. dried oregano

1   tbsp. all-purpose flour

1   tbsp. ground cumin

1½   cups beef stock

  Kosher salt and freshly ground black pepper, to taste

SERVES 4

1 Place all of the chiles in a bowl and cover with boiling water; let sit until softened, about 30 minutes. Remove chiles from water; discard stems and seeds. Transfer chiles to a blender along with soaking liquid and purée until smooth, at least 30 seconds. Set chile purée aside.

2 Heat bacon fat in a 6-qt. saucepan over medium-high. Add beef and pork and cook, stirring occasionally, until lightly browned all over, about 12 minutes. Using a wooden spoon, push meat to the perimeter of the pan and add garlic and onion to the center of the pan; cook, stirring, until soft, about 2 minutes. Add oregano, flour, and cumin, stir ingredients together, and cook until fragrant, about 2 minutes. Add reserved chile purée and stock and bring to a boil; reduce heat to medium-low and cook, covered partially and stirring occasionally, until meat is very tender and sauce is reduced slightly, about 1 hour. Season with salt and pepper, ladle into bowls, and serve.

Different iterations of this robust dish are eaten throughout the Republic of Georgia, some of them quite soupy and others served almost dry. The combination of salt-cured plums, hot chiles, and fresh herbs is typical of the bold, contrasting flavors popular in the Kakheti region of the country. Chinese pickled plums are easier to track down at specialty markets than Georgian ones and are a good substitute.

VEAL & SOUR PLUM STEW

¼	cup extra-virgin olive oil
2	lb. boneless veal shoulder, trimmed and cut into 2″ pieces
	Kosher salt and freshly ground black pepper, to taste
4	cloves garlic, finely chopped
1	large yellow onion, thinly sliced
1	small red Holland chile, stemmed, seeded, and finely chopped
¼	cup tomato paste
1	tsp. ground allspice
½	tsp. hot paprika
12	Georgian or Chinese jarred pickled plums, rinsed and drained
3	cups chicken stock
⅓	cup finely chopped fresh cilantro
¼	cup finely chopped fresh mint
¼	cup finely chopped scallions
2	tbsp. finely chopped fresh tarragon
	Country bread, for serving (optional)

SERVES 6-8

Heat oil in an 8-qt. saucepan over medium-high. Season veal with salt and pepper and cook, turning as needed, until browned, about 10 minutes. Add garlic, onion, and chile and cook, stirring occasionally, until golden, 8–10 minutes. Stir in tomato paste, allspice, and paprika and cook until slightly caramelized, about 2 minutes. Add plums and stock and bring to a boil. Reduce heat to medium and cook, covered, stirring occasionally, until veal is tender, 1–1½ hours. Stir in cilantro, mint, scallions, tarragon, salt, and pepper. Ladle stew into bowls and serve with bread.

DRIZZLED GARNISHES

A small drizzle of a flavorful oil, dressing, or sauce can add extra zing and style to a soup. There are many oils to choose from, including nut, avocado, and coconut, as well as extra-virgin olive oil and oils infused with lemon, lime, or blood orange. These poured toppings can be added just before serving or put in a small pitcher or gravy bowl and drizzled to taste at the table.

OILS For Mediterranean-style soups, consider a drizzle of extra-virgin olive oil or one of the many infused oils that contrast with or reflect the flavors of the soup. For example, rosemary and garlic–infused oil for a bean soup or a minestrone, blood orange–infused oil for a carrot soup, and lemon-infused oil for a seafood soup. For many soups with an Asian twist, toasted sesame oil, hot chile oil, and coconut oil are good choices, depending upon the flavor and other ingredients of the soup.

MUSHROOM SOY SAUCE Look no further for a serious dose of liquid umami. Mushroom "soy" sauce is made from nothing more than white button mushrooms and sea salt. The secret is to toss the mushrooms with the salt, let them sit for an hour, and then wrap the mushrooms in cheesecloth and squeeze to extract as much liquid as possible. Voilà! You have an earthy sauce ready for finishing a lentil-and-mushroom soup or a hot-and-sour soup.

HOT SAUCES In addition to the classic Tabasco sauce, there are an ever increasing number of hot sauces on the market ranging from mildly to intensely hot. These can be added to taste at the table.

GGS (GARLIC, GINGER & SHALLOT) DRESSING The piquant combination of rice vinegar, garlic, ginger, and shallots is versatile enough to enliven a basic miso soup or a hot-and-sour Thai *tom yum* soup.

SAGE BROWN BUTTER Give autumn vegetable soups made from butternut squash or winter roots a pop of flavor with a drizzle of nutty brown butter fragranced with fresh sage leaves. Simply melt butter in a small pan, add sage leaves, and cook to a toasty brown. The sizzled sage is also great crumbled over the soup.

CRÈME FRAÎCHE Flavor crème fraîche with finely chopped fresh herbs, such as tarragon or basil, or a pinch of spice, like cumin, coriander, or even curry, before drizzling or spooning it atop a vegetable- or legume-based soup.

Known in Hungary as *palócleves,* this satisfying soup takes advantage of the iconic Hungarian flavor combination of hot paprika and tangy sour cream. Tender lamb shoulder is cooked with wax beans and potatoes in an aromatic broth of garlic and paprika before rich sour cream is whisked in as a tangy counterpoint.

LAMB SOUP WITH SOUR CREAM

1/3   cup canola oil

10   oz. boneless lamb shoulder, trimmed and cut into 1/2″ pieces

Kosher salt and freshly ground black pepper, to taste

4   cloves garlic, finely chopped

2   bay leaves

1   large yellow onion, finely chopped

2   tbsp. Hungarian hot paprika

4   oz. russet potato, peeled and cut into 1/2″ pieces

4   oz. yellow wax or green beans, cut into 1″ pieces

3/4   cup sour cream, plus more to garnish

2   tbsp. flour

1   tbsp. coarsely chopped fresh dill, to garnish

SERVES 4-6

1 Heat oil in a 6-qt. saucepan over medium-high. Season lamb with salt and pepper and cook, stirring occasionally, until browned, about 8 minutes. Using a slotted spoon, transfer lamb to a bowl and set aside. Add garlic, bay leaves, onion, salt, and pepper to pan and cook, stirring occasionally, until garlic and onion are soft, about 15 minutes. Add reserved lamb, the paprika, and 4 cups water and bring to a boil. Reduce heat to medium-low; cover and cook, stirring occasionally, until lamb is slightly tender, about 20 minutes. Stir in potatoes and beans and simmer until lamb and vegetables are fully cooked, about 15 minutes more.

2 Whisk sour cream and flour in a bowl until smooth. Stir mixture into soup and cook until slightly thickened, about 10 minutes. Ladle soup into bowls and garnish with a dollop of sour cream and a sprinkling of dill.

The Pakistani recipe for *dumbay ki nihari* uses a home-blended garam masala for its defining sweet-spicy-bitter flavor profile. *Nihari* is derived from the Arabic word *nahaar,* or "day," which makes sense considering the long, slow cooking required to tenderize the meat and coax the thickening agents from the lamb bones. The result is a robust stew brightened with cilantro, ginger, citrus, and chile.

PAKISTANI SLOW-COOKED LAMB STEW

FOR THE GARAM MASALA

- 2 tbsp. poppy seeds
- 1 tbsp. coriander seeds
- 1 tsp. cumin seeds
- 1 tsp. fennel seeds
- ½ tsp. whole black peppercorns
- ¼ tsp. freshly grated nutmeg
- 5 whole cloves
- 3 green cardamom pods
- 1 black cardamom pod
- 1 star anise
- 1 stick cinnamon, halved

FOR THE STEW

- 1 cup canola oil
- 1 medium yellow onion, very thinly sliced
- 3 lamb shanks, halved crosswise (ask your butcher to do this)
- 1 tbsp. cayenne pepper
- 2 cloves garlic, mashed into a paste

- 1 3″ piece ginger, peeled (1″ mashed into a paste and 2″ julienned, to garnish)
- Kosher salt, to taste
- ¼ cup all-purpose flour
- 2 tbsp. ghee, melted
- Coarsely chopped fresh cilantro, lemon or lime wedges, and finely chopped Thai chiles, to garnish
- Naan bread, for serving (optional)

SERVES 4

1 Make the garam masala: Purée poppy seeds and 1 tbsp. water into a paste in a spice grinder, then transfer to a bowl. Wipe spice grinder dry and grind remaining spices into a powder; stir into poppy seed paste and set aside.

2 Make the stew: Heat oil and onion in a 6-qt. saucepan over medium. Cook, stirring occasionally, until onion is caramelized, about 25 minutes. Using a slotted spoon, transfer onion to a bowl and set aside. Discard all but ¼ cup oil from the pan. Add lamb shanks and cook, turning as needed, until browned, 8–10 minutes. Stir in reserved garam masala, the cayenne, garlic and ginger pastes, and salt and cook until fragrant, 1–2 minutes. Add 3 cups water and bring to a boil. Reduce heat to medium-low; cover and cook, stirring occasionally, until lamb meat has fallen off the bone, 5½–6 hours. Using tongs, transfer lamb to a bowl and keep warm.

3 Combine flour, ghee, and ¼ cup water in a bowl and add to pan. Cook until sauce is thickened, about 15 minutes. Return lamb to pan.

4 Ladle stew into bowls and garnish with the reserved onion, julienned ginger, the cilantro, lemon or lime wedges, and finely chopped chiles. Serve with naan.

Subtly sweet cauliflower gets a jolt of flavor with Middle Eastern spices and *harissa* (Tunisian hot sauce) in this chunky stew. The cauliflower stems are sautéed in the aromatics, while the florets are broiled and added at the end for a textural contrast.

LAMB & CAULIFLOWER STEW WITH HARISSA

5   tbsp. extra-virgin olive oil

4   tbsp. unsalted butter, melted

2   lb. boneless lamb shoulder, trimmed and cut into 2″ pieces

    Kosher salt and freshly ground black pepper, to taste

5   cloves garlic, finely chopped

3   plum tomatoes, finely chopped

2   large red onions, finely chopped

½   head cauliflower, cut into large florets, stems peeled and finely chopped

⅓   cup dry white wine

¼   cup tomato paste

2   tsp. ground cumin

1   tsp. ground cinnamon

5   cups lamb stock or Brown Chicken Stock (page 214)

2   tbsp. cornstarch mixed with 2 tbsp. cold water

⅓   cup harissa

8   pitted dates, coarsely chopped

½   tsp. smoked paprika

¼   cup sliced almonds, toasted, to garnish

SERVES 4–6

1 Heat oil and 2 tbsp. butter in a 6-qt. saucepan over medium-high. Season lamb with salt and pepper. Working in batches, cook lamb, turning as needed, until browned, about 20 minutes. Transfer lamb to a plate and set aside. Add garlic, tomatoes, onions, and finely chopped cauliflower stems to pan and cook until golden, 8–10 minutes. Add wine, tomato paste, cumin, and cinnamon and cook until mixture is fragrant and wine has evaporated, 2–3 minutes. Add reserved lamb and the stock and bring to a boil. Reduce heat to medium-low and cook, stirring occasionally, until lamb is very tender, about 2 hours. Stir in cornstarch mixture and return to a boil. Reduce heat to medium and stir in harissa, dates, salt, and pepper; cook for 5 minutes more.

2 Heat oven broiler. Combine remaining butter, the smoked paprika, salt, and pepper in a bowl. Place cauliflower florets on a baking sheet and toss with paprika butter. Broil, stirring as needed, until cauliflower is slightly charred and chewy, about 10 minutes. Ladle stew into bowls and garnish with charred cauliflower florets and the almonds.

WHY STEWS TASTE BETTER THE NEXT DAY

It's an old wives' tale that's actually true: Stews taste better when they've been left to snooze in the fridge overnight. But why? What magical, microscopic process is going on inside that pot? Actually, there are a few. The meat becomes juicier because its ability to hold moisture is dependent on temperature. Meat fibers contract and shrink when heated, limiting their carrying capacity. But if the meat is left to cool overnight in the stewing liquid, the fibers relax and allow the now-flavored moisture back in. The meat not only becomes more tender but also absorbs the other flavors of the ingredients with which it was cooked.

The properties of cooked spices contribute to the more complex, rounded flavor, as well. When most spices are cooked, they initially have an aggressive flavor, which can lead to a disharmonious dish. But when left to sit, the spices begin to break down and mingle with one another, creating that "married" flavor we seek.

In short, the overnight rest is what allows a stew to go from an assortment of individual tastes—meats, vegetables, liquids, and spices—to something far more unified . . . and delicious.

Birria, a spicy specialty of the Mexican state of Jalisco, is cooked slowly to ensure that the meat becomes fork-tender and the tomatillo broth is infused with a rich, meaty flavor. If you can't find or don't like goat, use bone-in pork shoulder in its place.

GOAT BIRRIA

1 dried guajillo chile, stemmed and seeded

1 cup boiling water

8 tomatillos, husked and cored

5 cloves garlic, unpeeled

1 medium white onion, halved (one half finely chopped)

1 serrano chile, stemmed

¼ cup cider vinegar

2 tsp. dried oregano, preferably Mexican

½ tsp. ground cinnamon, preferably Mexican

½ tsp. ground cumin

¼ tsp. freshly ground black pepper

1 2″ piece ginger, peeled and thinly sliced

2 tbsp. canola oil

3 lb. bone-in goat or pork shoulder, cut into 3″ pieces (ask your butcher to do this)

Kosher salt, to taste

1½ cups chicken stock

½ cup coarsely chopped fresh cilantro

Lime wedges, for serving

Corn tortillas, warmed, for serving (optional)

SERVES 6-8

1 Heat a 6-qt. saucepan over medium-high. Add guajillo chile and cook, flipping once, until lightly toasted, 3–4 minutes. Transfer to a blender, add the boiling water, and let sit until soft, about 30 minutes.

2 Meanwhile, return saucepan to medium-high and cook tomatillos, garlic, whole onion half, and serrano chile, turning as needed, until charred, 12–15 minutes. Peel garlic and transfer to blender with remaining charred vegetables. Add vinegar, oregano, cinnamon, cumin, pepper, and ginger; purée until smooth. Set chile sauce aside.

3 Add oil to saucepan and heat over medium-high. Season goat with salt. Working in batches, cook goat, turning as needed, until browned, 18–20 minutes. Using a slotted spoon, transfer to a bowl and set aside. Add finely chopped onion and cook until soft, 2–3 minutes. Add reserved chile sauce and simmer until thickened, 4–6 minutes. Return goat to pan, add stock, and bring to a boil. Reduce heat to medium; cover and cook, stirring occasionally, until goat is tender, about 2 hours. Using a slotted spoon, transfer goat to a cutting board. Let cool slightly, then shred meat, discarding bones, and return to pan. Stir in cilantro. Serve with lime wedges and tortillas.

CHICKEN
& POULTRY

For his rustic gumbo, New Orleans chef Donald Link makes his roux with the same oil he uses to fry the chicken, which he later shreds and adds to the pot along with slices of his homemade andouille sausage.

FRIED CHICKEN & ANDOUILLE GUMBO

1¼	cups plus 2 tbsp. canola oil
1	3½–4-lb. chicken, cut into 8 pieces
	Kosher salt, to taste
2½	tsp. freshly ground black pepper
2	cups flour
1½	tsp. dark chile powder
1½	tsp. filé powder
1	tsp. cayenne pepper
1	tsp. ground white pepper
1	tsp. paprika
3	cloves garlic, finely chopped
3	ribs celery, finely chopped
1	green bell pepper, stemmed, seeded, and finely chopped
1	jalapeño chile, stemmed and finely chopped
1	poblano chile, stemmed, seeded, and finely chopped
1	yellow onion, finely chopped
12	cups chicken stock
1	lb. andouille sausage, halved and sliced ½″ thick
12	oz. okra, sliced ½″ thick
	Sliced scallions, to garnish
	Cooked white rice, for serving

SERVES 6–8

1 Heat 1¼ cups oil in an 8-qt. Dutch oven until a deep-fry thermometer reads 350°F. Season chicken with salt and 1 tsp. black pepper; toss with ½ cup flour, shaking off excess. Working in batches, fry chicken until golden and transfer to paper towels to drain.

2 Whisk remaining flour into oil in pot until smooth. Heat over medium-low and cook, whisking constantly, until color of roux is dark chocolate, 1–1½ hours. Add remaining black pepper, the chile and filé powders, cayenne, white pepper, paprika, garlic, celery, bell pepper, jalapeño, poblano, and onion and cook until vegetables are soft, 10–12 minutes. Stir in stock and bring to a boil. Reduce heat to medium-low and cook, stirring occasionally and skimming fat as needed, until gumbo is slightly thickened, about 30 minutes. Add reserved chicken and cook until chicken is cooked through, about 45 minutes. Add andouille and cook until chicken is falling off the bone, about 1 hour. Using tongs, transfer chicken to a cutting board and let cool slightly; shred chicken, discarding skin and bones, and return to pot.

3 Heat remaining oil in a 12″ skillet over medium-high. Cook okra until golden brown and slightly crisp, 8–10 minutes. Stir okra into gumbo and cook for 15 minutes more. Ladle gumbo into bowls and garnish with scallions. Serve with rice.

SHADES OF ROUX

A roux (pronounced "roo") is what gives a gumbo its characteristic texture and intensity. The deep brown roux that forms the base of a gumbo is different from the white roux used to thicken a béchamel sauce or the blond roux used for chowders or cream soups. In the case of a white roux, equal weights of butter and flour are cooked together just long enough to rid the mixture of any raw flour flavor while remaining ivory white. A blond roux is cooked just until slightly darker.

A proper gumbo roux is more work-intensive, but the benefits are worth it. Whisk your flour into a pot containing an equal weight of heated oil or a rendered fat like lard or schmaltz. Reduce the heat from high to medium and stir the mixture vigorously. Continue to stir and scrape the sides and stir some more. You'll see the roux progress from pale to butterscotch to nut brown to dark chocolate in color, and it will start giving off a tantalizing burnt-popcorn aroma. This can take 1–1½ hours, which some Cajun cooks say is best spent stirring with one hand and drinking beer with the other. The reason for cooking the roux so long is threefold: It develops a deep, caramelized flavor; the darker color is better looking in the gumbo; and the prolonged cooking splits starch chains, making the roux less efficient at thickening but slower to congeal as the gumbo cools.

If your arm isn't up for this stove-side exercise, you can also make the roux in the oven. After whisking the flour into the fat, simply transfer the uncovered pot to a 350°F oven and bake the roux until it reaches the desired darkness, 1½–2 hours.

Tom ka gai is on just about every Thai takeout menu in the United States, making it almost as much a classic here as it is in Thailand. Its brilliance lies in the perfect balance of flavors—salty, sour, spicy, sweet, and umami—attained with only a quick simmer. Cooking it from scratch takes surprisingly little time and gives the dish the freshness found in homes and street stalls throughout Bangkok.

THAI COCONUT & CHICKEN SOUP

8   cups chicken stock

8   sprigs fresh cilantro, lower stems trimmed and reserved, tender stems and leaves reserved to garnish

5   kaffir lime leaves, coarsely chopped

1   stalk lemongrass, trimmed, smashed, and coarsely chopped

1   2″ piece ginger, unpeeled and thinly sliced

6   white button mushrooms, trimmed and thinly sliced

3   small red Thai chiles, halved lengthwise, or 1 serrano chile, stemmed and thinly sliced

2   boneless, skinless chicken breasts, thinly sliced

1   tbsp. packed brown sugar

1   14-oz. can coconut milk

3   tbsp. fresh lime juice, plus wedges for serving

2   tbsp. fish sauce

8   cherry tomatoes, halved

2   scallions, thinly sliced on the bias

    Hot chile oil, to garnish (optional)

SERVES 6–8

1 Combine stock, lower stems of cilantro, the lime leaves, lemongrass, and ginger in a 6-qt. saucepan and bring to a simmer over medium-high heat. Reduce heat to medium-low and cook for 15 minutes.

2 Strain stock through a fine-mesh sieve set over a bowl and discard solids; return stock to pan. Add mushrooms, chiles, and chicken; return to a simmer over medium-high. Simmer until chicken is cooked through, 2–4 minutes. Stir in sugar and coconut milk and return to a simmer. Stir in lime juice and fish sauce and ladle soup into bowls. Garnish with tender cilantro stems and leaves, tomatoes, and scallions and drizzle with hot chile oil. Serve with lime wedges.

Bold North African seasonings infuse this easy-to-make chicken and pasta soup. A mix of warm spices, garlic paste, and ginger paste is cooked with caramelized onions, releasing a potent fragrance. Preserved lemon rind is stirred in just before serving so its salty sweetness is not lost.

CHICKEN SOUP WITH ORZO & PRESERVED LEMON

3 tbsp. extra-virgin olive oil

1 small yellow onion, finely chopped

½ tsp. ground coriander

½ tsp. ground cumin

2 cloves garlic, mashed into a paste

1 1½" piece ginger, peeled and mashed into a paste

2 sticks cinnamon

1 bay leaf

8 cups chicken stock

¾ cup orzo pasta

2 boneless, skinless chicken breasts, cut into ½" pieces

½ cup finely chopped fresh flat-leaf parsley

 Rind of 1 preserved lemon, thinly sliced

 Kosher salt and freshly ground black pepper, to taste

SERVES 6-8

Heat oil in a 6-qt. saucepan over medium-high. Add onion and cook until caramelized, 20 minutes. Stir in coriander, cumin, garlic and ginger pastes, cinnamon, and bay leaf and cook until fragrant, 1–2 minutes. Add stock and bring to a boil. Add orzo and cook for 4 minutes. Add chicken and cook until pasta and chicken are cooked through, 3–4 minutes more. Stir in parsley, preserved lemon, salt, and pepper, and serve.

SMALL PASTAS FOR SOUPS

Small pastas contribute texture and heartiness to a wide variety of soups and stews. When including them in a soup, keep this in mind: The more delicate or thinner the soup, the smaller the pasta.

Many of the smallest soup pastas are used interchangeably, depending on what is on hand. *Acini di pepe* (peppercorns), *anelli* (thin rings), orzo, and *semi di melone* (melon seeds) are among the smallest pastas and are best paired with broth-based soups, like Italian wedding soup or avgolemono soup.

Childhood favorites like alphabet pasta and *stelline* (little stars) are great for kids and can be added to chicken or vegetable soups or creamy tomato soup.

In grown-up incarnations of chicken noodle soup, spiral egg noodles or short spaghetti-width *fideos* (Mexican broken vermicelli) can be added for body.

Denser pastas like *ditalini* (small tubes), *farfalline* (little butterflies), and *conchigliette* (small conch shells) stand up to heartier soups like minestrone and *pasta e fagioli*.

Nitza Villapol, the legendary Cuban cook and author, taught generations of islanders and exiles to make this savory chicken stew. It draws salty-sharp flavor from *alcaparrado* (a mix of pimiento-stuffed olives and capers) and sweetness from raisins.

CUBAN-STYLE CHICKEN STEW

¼ cup fresh lime juice

¼ cup fresh orange juice

3 cloves garlic, lightly smashed

1 3½–4-lb. chicken, quartered (backbone discarded or saved for stock)

Kosher salt and freshly ground black pepper, to taste

⅓ cup extra-virgin olive oil

1 large green bell pepper, stemmed, seeded, and thinly sliced

1 large white onion, thinly sliced

1 cup dry white wine

1 lb. russet potatoes, peeled and cut into 1" pieces

½ cup jarred alcaparrado or ⅓ cup pimiento-stuffed olives and 2 tbsp. capers

¼ cup raisins

1 8-oz. can tomato sauce

1 cup frozen peas, defrosted

SERVES 4–6

1 Combine lime and orange juices, garlic, chicken, salt, and pepper in a bowl. Cover with plastic wrap and set aside.

2 Heat oil in an 8-qt. saucepan over medium-high. Remove chicken from marinade and pat dry using paper towels; reserve marinade. Working in batches, cook chicken, flipping once, until browned, 8–10 minutes. Using tongs, transfer chicken to a plate and set aside. Add bell pepper and onion to pan and cook until soft, 6–8 minutes. Add wine; deglaze, stirring and scraping up browned bits from bottom of pan, and cook until reduced by half, 5–7 minutes. Return chicken to pan and add reserved marinade, the potatoes, alcaparrado, raisins, tomato sauce, salt, pepper, and ½ cup water and bring to a boil. Reduce heat to medium-low and cook, covered, until chicken and potatoes are tender, about 45 minutes. Stir in peas, spoon stew into bowls, and serve.

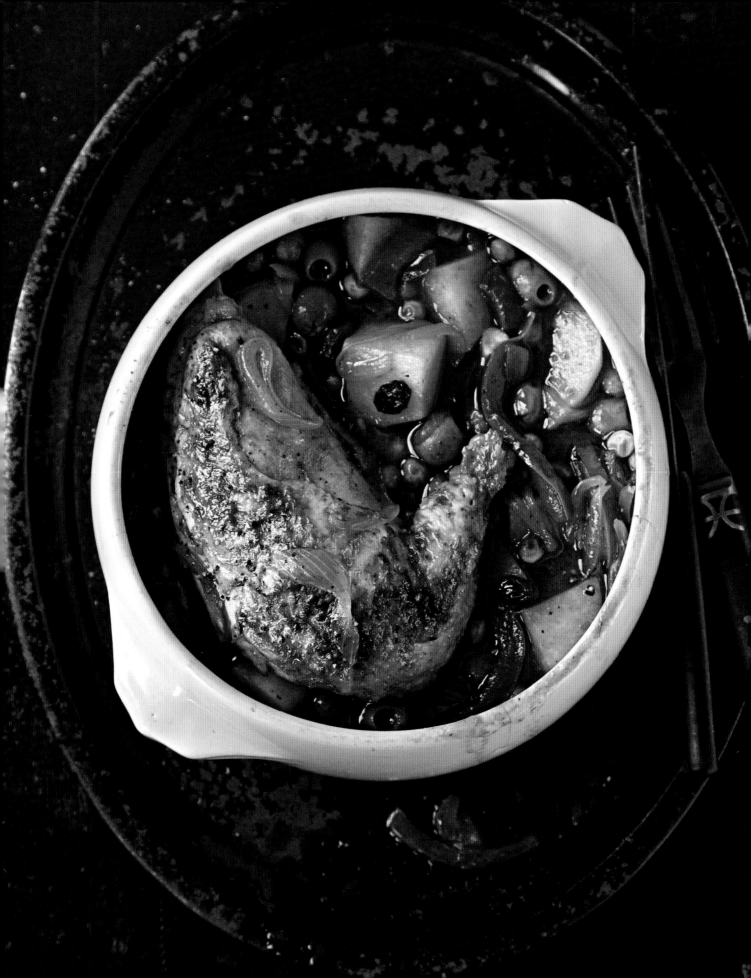

Escabeche, the delicately spiced and pleasantly tangy herb and citrus preparation typical of Mexico's Yucatán, makes a vibrant marinade and sauce for stewed chicken. The three citrus fruits called for in this recipe approximate the flavor of the Yucatán's sour oranges, which are difficult to find outside the region.

YUCATÁN-STYLE CHICKEN & ONION STEW

1	tbsp. dried oregano
1	tbsp. freshly ground black pepper
1	tbsp. ground coriander
1	tbsp. kosher salt
1½	tsp. ground cumin
¼	tsp. ground allspice
¼	tsp. ground cinnamon, preferably Mexican
¼	tsp. ground cloves
1	cup fresh grapefruit juice
1	cup fresh orange juice
¾	cup fresh lime juice
24	cloves garlic (4 finely chopped, 20 left whole)
2	3–4-lb. chickens, each cut into 8 pieces
4	Anaheim chiles, stemmed
2	tbsp. canola oil
5	medium white onions, halved and cut into ½"-thick slices
2	cups chicken stock
	Corn tortillas, warmed, for serving (optional)

SERVES 8

1 Whisk oregano, pepper, coriander, salt, cumin, allspice, cinnamon, and cloves in a bowl. Set half the spice mix aside and transfer remaining spice mix to a very large bowl. Whisk in grapefruit, orange, and lime juices and the finely chopped garlic. Add chicken pieces and toss to coat evenly in marinade. Cover with plastic wrap and chill for at least 4 hours.

2 Meanwhile, heat a cast-iron grill pan over medium-high. Grill whole garlic cloves and the chiles, turning as needed, until lightly charred, about 10 minutes for garlic and 25 minutes for chiles; transfer to a bowl and let cool. Remove chicken from marinade, reserving marinade. Working in batches, grill chicken, flipping once, until slightly charred, about 8 minutes. Transfer chicken to a plate and set aside.

3 Heat oil in a 6-qt. saucepan over medium. Add onions and sprinkle with reserved spice mix. Cook, stirring occasionally, until onions are golden, about 15 minutes. Stir in charred chiles and garlic, the reserved chicken and marinade, and the stock and bring to a boil. Reduce heat to medium-low and cook, covered, until chicken is cooked through, about 20 minutes. Uncover and continue cooking until liquid is slightly thickened, about 15 minutes. Ladle stew into bowls and serve with tortillas.

At the heart of this intriguing Persian-style chicken soup is a dumpling made of ground meat and chickpea flour. *Gundi* is as important to the Sephardic Jewish culinary culture of Iran as matzo ball soup is to the Ashkenazic kitchen of eastern and central Europe.

PERSIAN CHICKEN MEATBALL SOUP

¼ cup canola oil

1 lb. chicken wings

Kosher salt and freshly ground black pepper, to taste

3 carrots, coarsely chopped

3 medium yellow onions (2 coarsely chopped, 1 finely chopped)

2 cloves garlic, crushed

8 cups chicken stock

1 bay leaf

1½ lb. ground chicken

1½ cups chickpea flour

2½ tsp. ground turmeric

2 tsp. ground coriander

1½ tsp. baking soda

½ tsp. ground cardamom

SERVES 6

1 Heat 3 tbsp. oil in an 8-qt. saucepan over medium-high. Season wings with salt and pepper and cook, flipping once, until browned, about 13 minutes. Stir in carrots, coarsely chopped onions, and garlic and cook until vegetables are soft, about 8 minutes. Add stock, bay leaf, and salt and bring to a boil. Reduce heat to medium and cook until stock is slightly reduced, about 25 minutes. Strain stock through a fine-mesh sieve set over a bowl and discard solids; return stock to pan.

2 Heat remaining oil in a 12″ skillet over medium-high. Add finely chopped onion and cook until soft, 3–4 minutes. Transfer onion to a bowl and add remaining ingredients; mix until combined. Using wet hands, roll mixture into six 3″ balls.

3 Bring reserved stock to a simmer over medium heat. Gently add meatballs to stock and cook, partially covered, until meatballs are cooked through, about 17 minutes. Divide stock and meatballs between 6 bowls and serve.

Here's a soup that lets you make the most of your holiday leftovers. Think of it as a loose guide and let the contents of your refrigerator dictate the direction in which the flavors will go. Have a bit of uneaten roasted butternut squash or creamed spinach on hand? Add them, along with mashed potatoes for thickening. A garnish of leftover cranberry chutney is a good idea, too.

POST-THANKSGIVING TURKEY SOUP

6 cups turkey stock or Brown Chicken Stock (page 214)

1 turkey carcass, from roasted turkey, broken into pieces, or 2 turkey wings

2 tbsp. extra-virgin olive oil

1 tbsp. unsalted butter

2 carrots, coarsely chopped

2 cloves garlic, coarsely chopped

2 ribs celery, coarsely chopped

1 medium yellow onion, coarsely chopped

1 small turnip, peeled and coarsely chopped

2 sprigs fresh thyme

1 bay leaf

1 sprig fresh flat-leaf parsley

1 sprig fresh sage

2 cups finely shredded cooked turkey meat

1 cup mashed potatoes

½ cup canned evaporated milk

Kosher salt and freshly ground black pepper, to taste

¼ cup dried cranberries, to garnish

2 tbsp. chopped chives, to garnish

1 Bring stock and turkey carcass to a simmer in a large stockpot over medium-high. Remove from heat and skim excess fat, if needed. Keep covered until ready to use.

2 Heat oil and butter in an 8-qt. saucepan over medium-high. Cook carrots, garlic, celery, onion, and turnip, stirring occasionally, until golden, 10 minutes. Tie thyme, bay leaf, parsley, and sage into a bundle using butcher's twine and add to pan. Strain reserved turkey stock through a fine-mesh sieve set over a bowl and discard solids; return stock to pan and bring to a boil. Reduce heat to medium. Stir in shredded turkey and mashed potatoes and cook until soup is thickened, 30 minutes. Add evaporated milk and season with salt and pepper. Discard herb bundle. To serve, ladle soup into bowls and garnish with cranberries and chives.

SERVES 6–8

Preparing a Japanese hot pot, which calls for gently simmering ingredients in broth, is an art built on one simple rule: All the components must be added in a particular order to maximize flavor and texture. Here, the light, delicately flavored medley of mushrooms, meatballs, and vegetables is seasoned with soy sauce at the table.

JAPANESE MISO CHICKEN MEATBALL HOT POT

FOR THE MEATBALLS

- 1 lb. ground chicken
- 2 tbsp. cornstarch
- 1 tbsp. soy sauce
- 2 tsp. toasted sesame oil
- 2 scallions, finely chopped
- 1 clove garlic, mashed into a paste
- 1 2″ piece ginger, peeled and mashed into a paste

FOR THE BROTH

- 3 cups Ichiban Dashi (page 217)
- ⅓ cup miso
- ¼ cup sake
- 1 clove garlic, thinly sliced
- 1 1″ piece ginger, peeled and thinly sliced
- 1 small head Savoy cabbage, cored and cut into 2″ pieces
- 6 large shiitake mushrooms, stemmed and sliced ½″ thick
- 2 carrots, sliced ½″ thick on the bias
- 4 oz. enoki mushrooms, stems trimmed (optional)
- 6 scallions, trimmed and cut into 2″ pieces
- 2 cups baby spinach

  Soy sauce, for serving

SERVES 6–8

1 Make the meatballs: Mix ingredients in a bowl until combined. Using wet hands, roll mixture into twelve 1½ oz. balls and place on a parchment paper–lined baking sheet. Cover with plastic wrap and freeze for 20 minutes.

2 Make the broth: Combine dashi, miso, sake, garlic, and ginger in a Japanese hot pot or wide 6-qt. Dutch oven. Add cabbage evenly over bottom of hot pot and bring to a simmer over medium-high. Add shiitake mushrooms, carrots, and reserved meatballs in separate clusters over cabbage. Reduce heat to medium-low and cook, covered, until meatballs are just cooked, about 15 minutes. Uncover hot pot and add enoki mushrooms and scallions in separate bunches; cook, covered, 4–6 minutes. Uncover and add spinach in a bunch on one side of hot pot; cook, covered, until spinach is wilted, 1–2 minutes. Serve hot pot with soy sauce on the side.

This West African stew starts with a simple homemade peanut butter, which delivers a deep, subtly sweet richness to the dish. If pressed for time, substitute a commercial natural peanut butter (without stabilizers and sugar) to get the same silky texture and pure peanut flavor.

SENEGALESE PEANUT & CHICKEN STEW

2 cups shelled, skinned peanuts

¼ cup peanut oil

2 lb. boneless, skinless chicken thighs, cut into 1½″ pieces

Kosher salt and freshly ground black pepper, to taste

6 cloves garlic, finely chopped

1 large yellow onion, finely chopped

¼ cup tomato paste

1 habanero or Scotch bonnet chile, stemmed and finely chopped

1 bay leaf

4 cups chicken or vegetable stock

½ lb. small carrots, halved lengthwise

10 okra, halved lengthwise

2 medium sweet potatoes or 1 small butternut squash, peeled, halved, seeded, and cut into 1″ pieces

1 small head green cabbage, cut into 8 wedges, core left intact

¼ cup fresh lime juice

Cooked fonio (small West African grain) or white rice, for serving

Khouthia (hibiscus leaf conserve), for serving (optional)

SERVES 6–8

1 Heat oven to 350°F. Spread the peanuts on a baking sheet and roast, stirring occasionally, until golden brown, about 10 minutes. Let peanuts cool, then transfer to a food processor and purée into a smooth paste. Set ⅓ cup aside (refrigerate remaining peanut butter for another use for up to 2 weeks).

2 Heat oil in a 6-qt. Dutch oven over medium-high. Season chicken with salt and pepper and cook, flipping once, until browned, about 12 minutes. Using a slotted spoon, transfer chicken to a plate and set aside.

3 Add garlic and onion to the pan and cook, stirring occasionally, until soft, about 6 minutes. Add tomato paste and cook until slightly caramelized, about 2 minutes. Stir in reserved peanut butter, the chile, and bay leaf and cook until fragrant, 2–4 minutes. Stir in stock until sauce is smooth. Add reserved chicken, the carrots, okra, sweet potatoes, and cabbage and bring to a boil. Reduce heat to medium-low; partially cover and cook, stirring occasionally, until chicken and vegetables are tender, about 25 minutes. Using a slotted spoon, transfer chicken and vegetables to a serving bowl or platter. Simmer sauce, stirring often, until thickened, about 12 minutes. Stir in lime juice, salt, and pepper. Pour sauce over chicken and vegetables. Serve stew with fonio and khouthia on the side.

Pomegranate molasses, an intensely tart fruit syrup, brings sweet, sour, and bitter notes to this classic Iranian stew; look for it at Middle Eastern shops. Accompany the stew with basmati rice for soaking up the flavorful walnut-rich sauce.

IRANIAN CHICKEN & WALNUT STEW

1/4   **cup canola oil**

2   **lb. boneless, skinless chicken thighs, cut into 2 1/2" pieces**

   Kosher salt and freshly ground black pepper, to taste

1 1/2   **tbsp. ground turmeric**

1   **large white onion, thinly sliced**

2   **cups finely chopped spinach**

1 1/2   **lb. shelled walnuts**

2   **cups pomegranate molasses**

1/4   **cup sugar**

   Cooked basmati rice, for serving

   Sliced red onion, to garnish

SERVES 6-8

1 Heat oil in a 12" skillet over medium-high. Season chicken with salt and pepper. Working in batches, cook chicken, turning as needed, until browned, about 8 minutes. Using a slotted spoon, transfer chicken to a plate and set aside. Add turmeric and onion to skillet and cook until onion is soft, about 10 minutes. Add spinach and cook until wilted, about 1 minute. Remove from heat and set aside.

2 Purée walnuts in a food processor into a smooth paste, about 2 minutes. Transfer walnut paste to a 6-qt. Dutch oven and cook over medium-low, stirring occasionally, until fragrant, about 15 minutes. Raise heat to medium and stir in 8 cups water; simmer, skimming any oil that floats to the surface, until paste is light brown and thickened, about 2 hours. Add pomegranate molasses and sugar and cook until thickened once more, about 25 minutes. Add reserved chicken and onion-spinach mixture and cook until chicken is cooked through, about 30 minutes. Divide rice between bowls and ladle stew over. Garnish with red onion.

Versions of this hearty and filling chicken stew can be found in many Latin American countries. This Mexican-inspired take develops a smoky flavor from chipotle chiles in adobo. It can also be made with leftover chicken, pork, or beef.

CHIPOTLE CHICKEN & POTATO STEW

¼ cup canola oil

1½ lb. boneless, skinless chicken thighs

Kosher salt and freshly ground black pepper, to taste

1 carrot, coarsely chopped

1 red bell pepper, stemmed, seeded, and coarsely chopped

1 small white onion, coarsely chopped

1 cup coarsely chopped fresh or canned pineapple

1 tsp. dried thyme

1 tsp. ground cumin

6 cloves garlic, finely chopped

2 canned chipotle chiles in adobo sauce, finely chopped

1 jalapeño chile, quartered lengthwise

1 lb. Yukon gold potatoes, peeled and cut into ½″ pieces

4 cups chicken stock

3 sprigs fresh epazote or cilantro

1 15-oz. can whole peeled tomatoes, crushed by hand

3 tbsp. capers, rinsed and drained

Juice of 1 lime

SERVES 6–8

1 Heat oil in a 6-qt. saucepan over medium-high. Season chicken with salt and pepper. Working in batches, cook chicken, flipping once, until browned and cooked through, about 15 minutes. Using tongs, transfer to a plate and let cool. Finely shred meat, discarding skin and bones, and set aside.

2 Return pan to medium-high and cook carrot, bell pepper, and onion, stirring occasionally, until soft, about 8 minutes. Stir in pineapple, thyme, cumin, garlic, chipotles, and jalapeño and cook until fragrant, about 2 minutes. Add reserved shredded chicken, the potatoes, stock, epazote, and tomatoes and bring to a boil. Reduce heat to medium-low and cook, stirring occasionally, until potatoes are tender, about 30 minutes. Add capers and lime juice, season with salt and pepper, and serve.

A rich and complex tomatillo and chile base marries with warm spices and beer for this big-bowl crowd-pleaser. A dollop of cooling sour cream helps offset the heat.

GREEN CHICKEN & WHITE BEAN CHILI

1½ lb. tomatillos (about 10), husked and rinsed

4   serrano chiles (3 stemmed, 1 thinly sliced, to garnish)

3   poblano chiles, stemmed

1   cup chicken stock

1   cup coarsely chopped fresh cilantro leaves and tender stems, plus more leaves to garnish

1   cup sour cream, plus more to garnish

Kosher salt and freshly ground black pepper, to taste

¼   cup extra-virgin olive oil

1   lb. ground chicken

1   large yellow onion, finely chopped

2   tsp. ground cumin

1½ tsp. ancho chile powder

1   tsp. ground coriander

6   cloves garlic, finely chopped

1   12-oz. bottle Mexican-style lager, such as Corona or Dos Equis

1   15-oz. can white beans, such as navy or cannellini, rinsed and drained

Lime wedges, for serving

Tortilla chips, for serving (optional)

SERVES 6

1 Heat oven broiler. Place tomatillos, stemmed serranos, and poblanos on a foil-lined baking sheet and broil, turning as needed, until blackened, about 10 minutes. Transfer to a bowl and cover with plastic wrap. When poblanos are cool, peel, seed, and coarsely chop; set aside. Peel tomatillos and serranos and transfer to a blender. Add stock, cilantro, sour cream, salt, and pepper; purée until smooth and set aside.

2 Heat 2 tbsp. oil in a 6-qt. Dutch oven over medium-high. Cook chicken, stirring and breaking up into large clumps, until browned, 6–8 minutes. Push chicken to edges of pot and add onion; cook until golden, 5–6 minutes. Stir in remaining oil, cumin, chile powder, coriander, and garlic and cook until fragrant, 1–2 minutes. Add beer; deglaze, stirring and scraping up browned bits from bottom of pan, and cook until reduced by half, 8 minutes. Add reserved poblanos, sauce, the beans, salt, and pepper and simmer until chili is thickened, 30 minutes. Ladle chili into bowls and garnish with sour cream, sliced serrano, and cilantro. Serve with lime wedges and tortilla chips.

Sancocho, from the Spanish for "parboil," is a popular soup in many Latin American and Caribbean countries. While specific elements change from place to place, the dish always involves some sort of meat and a mix of starchy vegetables. This version comes from Puerto Rico and calls for chicken and a hearty medley of carrots, potatoes, plantains, and spaghetti noodles.

CHICKEN & ROOT VEGETABLE SOUP

2 tbsp. canola oil

3 cloves garlic, crushed

1 large yellow onion, finely chopped

1 plum tomato, cored, seeded, and finely chopped

10 cups chicken stock

8 bone-in chicken thighs, skin removed

8 sprigs fresh cilantro, plus more to garnish

½ lb. waxy potatoes, peeled and cut into 1" pieces

3 carrots, peeled and sliced ¼" thick

1 large green plantain, peeled and cut into 1" pieces

2 oz. spaghetti, broken in half

Kosher salt and freshly ground black pepper, to taste

SERVES 6-8

1 Heat oil in an 8-qt. saucepan over medium. Add garlic, onion, and tomato and cook until soft, about 8 minutes. Add stock, chicken, and cilantro and cook for 20 minutes. Add potatoes, carrots, and plantain and cook until chicken and vegetables are tender, about 25 minutes.

2 Using tongs, transfer chicken to a cutting board and let cool slightly. Shred chicken into bite-size pieces, discarding bones. Return chicken to pan. Stir in spaghetti and cook until al dente, about 8 minutes. Season with salt and pepper. Ladle soup into bowls, garnish with cilantro, and serve.

SEAFOOD
& CHOWDERS

This simple fish soup takes its name from *kakavi,* the traditional three-legged cooking vessel used by Greek fishermen since ancient times. Ingredients of this soup vary depending on the day's catch. The addition of eel here lends body and flavor to the broth.

KAKAVIA

1/3 cup extra-virgin olive oil

4 sprigs fresh flat-leaf parsley

2 bay leaves

2 sprigs fresh oregano

1 small yellow onion, halved

1/2 bulb fennel, plus 3 fronds to garnish

1 1/2 lb. eel or monkfish, cleaned and cut into 4" pieces

2 1-lb. sea bass or red snappers, cleaned and filleted, bones and heads reserved

2 cups dry white wine

2 cloves garlic, finely chopped

1/2 tsp. Aleppo pepper or 1/8 tsp. crushed red chile flakes

3 Yukon gold potatoes, peeled and cut into 1" pieces

2 carrots, peeled and cut into 1" pieces

2 medium zucchini, cut into 2" pieces

2 tbsp. fresh lemon juice

Kosher salt, to taste

SERVES 4-6

1 Heat 5 tbsp. oil in a 6-qt. saucepan over high. Cook parsley, bay leaves, oregano, onion, and fennel bulb, stirring occasionally, for 4 minutes. Add eel, sea bass bones and heads, 1 1/2 cups wine, and 9 cups water and bring to a boil. Reduce heat to medium-high and cook, stirring occasionally and skimming as needed, until stock reduces to 7 cups, about 1 hour. Strain stock through a fine-mesh sieve set over a bowl, pressing on the bones to expel as much liquid as possible; discard solids and set stock aside.

2 Heat remaining oil, the garlic, and Aleppo pepper in a 4-qt. saucepan over medium and cook, stirring occasionally, until garlic is soft, about 2 minutes. Add remaining wine and reserved stock, the potatoes, carrots, and zucchini and bring to a boil. Reduce heat to medium and cook until vegetables are tender, about 15 minutes. Halve sea bass fillets crosswise and add them to the stock; cook until fillets are opaque, about 4 minutes. Gently stir in lemon juice and salt so as not to break up the fish. Ladle soup into bowls and garnish with fennel fronds.

Mussels and oats may not sound like a go-to combination, but they are in Scotland—and for good reason. Brose, the Scottish word for a porridge of oats and hot water, is often eaten with salt and butter. Here, in this traditional recipe, a touch of Scottish oatmeal thickens and adds body to the broth while infusing it with a nutty flavor.

CREAMY MUSSEL BROSE

¼ cup finely ground
Scottish oatmeal

12 tbsp. unsalted butter

4 cloves garlic, smashed

4 small yellow onions
(2 coarsely chopped,
2 finely chopped)

3 lb. mussels, scrubbed
and debearded

2 cups dry white wine

2 sprigs fresh flat-leaf parsley

Kosher salt and freshly
ground black pepper, to taste

2 cups heavy cream

Coarsely chopped chives,
to garnish

SERVES 6

1 Heat oatmeal in an 8-qt. saucepan over medium. Cook, stirring occasionally, until lightly toasted, 1–2 minutes. Transfer oatmeal to a bowl and set aside.

2 Add 6 tbsp. butter to pan and melt over medium-high. Cook garlic and coarsely chopped onion until soft, 3–4 minutes. Add mussels, wine, parsley, salt, pepper, and 1 cup water and bring to a boil. Reduce heat to medium and cook, covered, until mussel shells open, 5–7 minutes. Using a slotted spoon, transfer mussels to a bowl and let cool. Strain broth through a fine-mesh sieve into a bowl and set aside. When mussels are cool, reserve 24 in their shells; shell the remaining mussels, place in a bowl, and set aside.

3 Wipe pan clean, add remaining butter, and melt over medium-high. Cook finely chopped onion until soft, 3–4 minutes. Add reserved broth and the cream and bring to a boil. Whisk in reserved oatmeal and cook until oats are tender and brose is thickened, 5–7 minutes. Stir in reserved shelled mussels and season with salt and pepper. Cook until heated through, 1–2 minutes more. Ladle brose into bowls and garnish with reserved mussels and the chives.

A stock made from fresh crab shells elevates this luxurious soup, though a commercial or homemade fish stock could be used in a pinch. The intensely flavorful stock is thickened with a light roux and balanced by toasty golden garlic and dry white wine.

GOLDEN GARLIC & DUNGENESS CRAB SOUP

¾ cup extra-virgin olive oil

12 cloves garlic, coarsely chopped

1 large shallot, finely chopped

1 cup dry white wine

½ cup rice flour or all-purpose flour

5 cups Dungeness crab stock or fish stock (page 216)

2 cups half-and-half

Kosher salt and freshly ground black pepper, to taste

1 cup grated Parmigiano-Reggiano

1 cup cooked Dungeness crabmeat, finely shredded

Fennel fronds, to garnish

SERVES 6

1 Combine oil and garlic in a 4-qt. saucepan. Bring to a simmer over medium and cook until garlic is golden, 3–4 minutes. Using a slotted spoon, transfer garlic to paper towels to drain and set aside.

2 Raise heat to medium-high; add shallot and cook until soft, 2–3 minutes. Add wine and cook until reduced by half, 3–4 minutes. Stir in flour and cook for 2 minutes. Whisk in stock, half-and-half, salt, and pepper and cook until slightly thickened, 8–10 minutes. Stir in half the Parmigiano. Divide soup between 6 bowls; top with reserved garlic, remaining Parmigiano, the crabmeat, and fennel fronds.

Datil chiles are unique to St. Augustine, Florida, where a large Minorcan population has been living since their original immigration there in the late 1700s. The chiles add heat and tang to this tomato-based clam chowder, but habaneros, which have a similar aromatic flavor, are a good alternative.

MINORCAN CLAM CHOWDER

1   cup bottled clam juice

1½   lb. hard-shell clams,
     such as littleneck or
     cherrystone, scrubbed

2   oz. salt pork, finely chopped

1   tbsp. extra-virgin olive oil

2   tsp. finely chopped
     fresh thyme

1   tsp. dried basil

½   tsp. dried marjoram

½   tsp. dried oregano

3   cloves garlic, finely chopped

1   bay leaf

1   datil or habanero chile,
     stemmed and finely chopped

1   green bell pepper, stemmed,
     seeded, and finely chopped

1   large yellow onion,
     finely chopped

3   cups fish stock (page 216)

3   plum tomatoes, chopped

1   28-oz. can whole peeled
     tomatoes, crushed by hand

1   lb. waxy potatoes, peeled
     and cut into ½″ pieces

     Kosher salt and freshly
     ground black pepper, to taste

     Crackers, for serving
     (optional)

SERVES 8

Bring clam juice to a boil in a 6-qt. saucepan over medium-high. Add clams and cook, covered, until shells open, 1–2 minutes. Transfer clams to a bowl and discard shells; reserve juice in another bowl. Add pork and oil to pan and cook over medium-high until pork is crisp, about 3 minutes. Add thyme, basil, marjoram, oregano, garlic, bay leaf, chile, bell pepper, and onion and cook until golden, 6–8 minutes. Add reserved clam juice, stock, and fresh and canned tomatoes and bring to a boil. Reduce heat to medium, add potatoes, and cook until tender, 25–30 minutes. Stir in reserved clams, salt, and pepper. Serve with crackers.

Maine chowder differs from other New England chowders in that it is not usually thickened with flour. The result is a lighter soup perfectly suited to highlight—not overpower—delicate Maine shrimp.

MAINE SHRIMP CHOWDER

3   lb. shrimp, preferably from Maine, shells and heads on

4   oz. slab bacon, cut into ¼″ pieces

3   medium russet potatoes, quartered lengthwise and sliced crosswise into ½″ pieces

1   large leek, white part only, cut into ¼″ pieces and rinsed

3   tbsp. unsalted butter

¾   cup heavy cream

Kosher salt and freshly ground black pepper, to taste

Pinch cayenne pepper

2   tsp. finely chopped chives, to garnish

SERVES 4

1 Peel shrimp and remove heads, reserving both for the shrimp stock. Transfer shrimp to a bowl, cover, and chill until ready to use. Place shrimp shells and heads in a large stockpot, add 10 cups cold water, and bring to a simmer over medium-high. Reduce heat to low and gently simmer for 5 minutes, skimming off any foam that rises to the surface. Strain stock through a fine-mesh sieve into a bowl and discard solids. Set aside.

2 Bring a 4-qt. saucepan of water to a simmer over medium-high. Blanch bacon for 1 minute, then drain and return bacon to pan over medium. Cook, stirring occasionally, until bacon releases some of its fat. Reduce heat to medium-low and stir in potatoes and leek; cover and cook, stirring occasionally, 5 minutes. Add 3 cups of the reserved shrimp stock (freeze remainder for another use) and bring to a simmer over medium; cook, covered, until potatoes are tender, 8–10 minutes. Keep chowder base warm.

3 Melt butter in a 12″ skillet over high. Add the chilled shrimp and the cream and bring to a boil; cook for 30 seconds. Stir shrimp mixture into reserved chowder base, cover, and let sit for 10 minutes before seasoning with salt, pepper, and cayenne. Ladle chowder into bowls, garnish with chives, and serve.

Conflicting theories exist on where Scotland's famed finnan haddie, or cold-smoked haddock, originated, with at least two northeastern villages vying for the honor. Here, this prized fish is used in a rich, hearty chowder that also includes clams.

FINNAN HADDIE CHOWDER

1	lb. finnan haddie (cold-smoked haddock), cut into 1″ pieces
2	tbsp. unsalted butter
1	small yellow onion, finely chopped
2	tbsp. flour
2½	cups bottled clam juice
1	bay leaf
1	sprig fresh thyme
1	lb. waxy potatoes, peeled and cut into ¼″ pieces
3	cups heavy cream
10	littleneck clams, scrubbed
3	tbsp. dry sherry
	Kosher salt, to taste
	Chervil leaves, to garnish

SERVES 6–8

Soak finnan haddie in a bowl of cold water for 30 minutes; drain. Melt butter in a 6-qt. saucepan over medium-high. Cook onion until soft, 3–4 minutes. Sprinkle in flour and cook for 2 minutes. Whisk in clam juice, bay leaf, and thyme and bring to a boil. Reduce heat to medium and cook until thickened, 18–20 minutes. Add potatoes and cream and simmer until potatoes are tender, about 15 minutes. Stir in reserved finnan haddie and the clams and cook until shells open, 8–10 minutes. Stir in sherry and salt; discard bay leaf and thyme. Ladle chowder into bowls and garnish with chervil.

SOUP THICKENERS

These thickening agents are the key to rich soups and can add heartiness to thin soups.

ROUX Made of equal parts flour and fat (usually butter or oil), a roux is cooked to varying shades depending on its use. The darker you cook the roux, the more flavor you gain and the more thickening power you lose. Once the roux has reached the desired color, stock or other liquid is whisked into it and the mixture is cooked to the desired thickness. (For more information on roux, see page 45.)

STARCH A slurry is made by dissolving cornstarch, potato starch, or arrowroot with a small quantity of water to achieve a creamlike consistency. The slurry is then whisked into the soup and the soup is brought to a boil, thickening almost immediately.

GELATIN A good way to thicken a clear soup and give it a velvety mouthfeel is to add a large bone or two to the simmering broth. A calf's foot is a good choice, as it releases a generous amount of natural gelatin into the liquid as it simmers. The resulting soup has more body than a plain broth and the gelatin does not cloud it.

PASTA & RICE One of the simplest ways to thicken a soup is to cook pasta or rice directly in it. When the pasta or rice cooks, it releases starch that thickens the soup.

In Norway, all the parts of the cod—from cheeks to liver—come together in creamy *fiskesuppe,* a warming dinnertime staple. Feel free to substitute mahimahi, salmon, scallops, or shrimp for the cod.

NORWEGIAN COD & ROOT VEGETABLE CHOWDER

6   tbsp. unsalted butter

4   cloves garlic,
    coarsely chopped

2   ribs celery, coarsely chopped

1   green bell pepper, stemmed,
    seeded, and coarsely chopped

1   small leek, sliced ¼″ thick
    and rinsed

1   small onion, coarsely chopped

    Kosher salt and black pepper,
    to taste

4   medium new potatoes,
    peeled and cut into 1″ pieces

2   medium carrots, sliced
    ¼″ thick

1   large parsnip, peeled
    and coarsely chopped

1   small celeriac, peeled
    and coarsely chopped

3   cups fish stock (page 216)

2   cups milk

1   cup heavy cream

1½ tbsp. Worcestershire sauce

2   lb. boneless, skinless cod
    fillet, cut into 2″ pieces

⅓   cup coarsely chopped
    fresh dill, plus more
    to garnish

¼   cup coarsely chopped
    fresh flat-leaf parsley

    Juice of 1 lemon

    Crusty bread, for serving

Melt butter in a 6-qt. saucepan over medium-high. Add garlic, celery, bell pepper, leek, onion, salt, and pepper and cook, stirring occasionally, until soft, 8–10 minutes. Add potatoes, carrots, parsnip, celeriac, stock, milk, cream, and Worcestershire and bring to a boil. Reduce heat to medium and cook, stirring occasionally, until vegetables are tender, about 25 minutes. Add cod and continue to cook, stirring gently, until fish is cooked through, 6–8 minutes. Stir in dill, parsley, lemon juice, salt, and pepper. Garnish with additional dill. Serve with bread.

SERVES 6–8

A generous amount of homemade aïoli, pungent with garlic and rich with olive oil, is whisked into the wine-and-saffron-flavored broth of this satisfying French stew from Marseille. The resulting creamy consistency, combined with vibrant leek and tomato, complements the halibut and shrimp.

MARSEILLE-STYLE FISH STEW WITH AÏOLI

FOR THE AÏOLI

- 2 tsp. fresh lemon juice
- 1 clove garlic, finely chopped
- 1 egg yolk
  Kosher salt, to taste
- 1 cup extra-virgin olive oil

FOR THE SOUP

- ¼ cup extra-virgin olive oil
- 1 tsp. fennel seeds
- ¼ tsp. cayenne pepper
- 2 cloves garlic, crushed
- 2 leeks, white parts only, coarsely chopped and rinsed
- 2 plum tomatoes, quartered
- 2 small yellow onions, coarsely chopped
- 1 bay leaf
- 1½ cups dry white wine
- 4 cups fish stock (page 216)
- 2 lb. skinless firm white fish, such as halibut or monkfish, pin bones removed, cut into 2" pieces
- 10 oz. medium shrimp, peeled and deveined, tails removed
- ½ tsp. saffron threads
  Kosher salt and freshly ground black pepper, to taste
- 2 tbsp. finely chopped fresh flat-leaf parsley, to garnish
  Toasted baguette, for serving

SERVES 6

1 Make the aïoli: Whisk together lemon juice, garlic, egg yolk, and salt in a heatproof bowl set over a saucepan of simmering water until thickened, 2–3 minutes; transfer to a blender. With the motor running, drizzle in oil until sauce is emulsified. Transfer aïoli to a bowl and set aside.

2 Make the soup: Heat oil in a 6-qt. saucepan over medium. Add fennel seeds, cayenne, garlic, leeks, tomatoes, onions, and bay leaf and cook until soft, about 15 minutes. Add wine and cook until reduced by half, 4–5 minutes. Add stock and 2 cups water and bring to a boil. Reduce heat to medium and cook until stock is slightly reduced, 12–15 minutes. Strain stock through a fine-mesh sieve into a bowl and discard solids; return stock to saucepan over medium. Add fish, shrimp, saffron, salt, and pepper and cook until fish is firm and shrimp are pink, 2–3 minutes. Using a slotted spoon, divide fish and shrimp between 6 bowls.

3 Whisk ½ cup broth into aïoli then whisk aïoli mixture into pan. Cook broth until slightly thick, 4–5 minutes; ladle over fish. Garnish with parsley and serve with toasted baguette.

One taste of this chile-spiked mussel and shrimp stew from Senegal, which calls for both traditional palm oil and fish sauce, will convince you that it's a predecessor of Louisiana-style gumbo.

SENEGALESE OKRA & SEAFOOD STEW

12   **cups fish stock (page 216)**

4   **cups okra, sliced ½″ thick**

3   **bay leaves**

2   **medium yellow onions, coarsely chopped**

6   **tbsp. palm oil**

¼   **cup fish sauce**

2   **habanero or Scotch bonnet chiles, slit in half lengthwise**

1   **large eggplant or 4 small Thai eggplants, cut into 1″ chunks**

24   **mussels, scrubbed and debearded**

16   **medium shrimp, peeled and deveined, tails on**

    Freshly ground black pepper, to taste

    Cooked white rice or fonio (small West African grain), for serving

SERVES 6–8

1 Bring the stock to a boil in a 6-qt. saucepan. Reduce heat to medium-low and add okra, bay leaves, and onions. Cook, stirring occasionally, until okra is very tender and stock has reduced by one-quarter, about 1½ hours.

2 Stir palm oil, 3 tbsp. fish sauce, the chiles, and eggplant into the broth. Cook, stirring occasionally, until stew is thickened and okra falls apart, about 30 minutes.

3 Add mussels and shrimp and cook, covered, until mussel shells open and shrimp are pink, about 4 minutes. Stir in remaining fish sauce and the pepper, and stew into bowls. Serve with rice.

The broth for this warming Icelandic soup gets its full-bodied flavor from langoustine shells before it is bolstered with cream and curry powder. The plump poached langoustine tail meat, plus whipped cream and chives, makes a dramatic—and delicious—garnish.

ICELANDIC LANGOUSTINE SOUP

2	lb. shell-on whole langoustines (European lobsters)
8	tbsp. unsalted butter
2	tbsp. extra-virgin olive oil
2	carrots, finely chopped
2	ribs celery, finely chopped
1	large yellow onion, finely chopped
2	tbsp. tomato paste
2	tsp. paprika
	Kosher salt and freshly ground black pepper, to taste
12	cups fish stock (page 216)
2	cloves garlic, finely chopped
1	tbsp. mild curry powder
1½	cups heavy cream
1	cup dry white wine
2	tbsp. finely chopped chives, to garnish

SERVES 4

1 Remove heads and shells from langoustines and lightly crush; chill tail meat until ready to use. Heat 1 tbsp. butter and the oil in an 8-qt. saucepan over medium-high. Cook heads and shells, carrots, celery, and half the onion until vegetables are soft, 6–8 minutes. Stir in tomato paste, paprika, salt, and pepper and cook for 2 minutes. Add stock and simmer until reduced by half, about 2 hours. Strain stock through a fine-mesh sieve into a bowl and discard solids; set aside.

2 Wipe pan clean and add 4 tbsp. butter; melt over medium. Cook remaining onion and the garlic until soft, 3–4 minutes. Stir in curry powder and cook for 1 minute. Add 1 cup cream and the wine and cook until reduced by half, about 20 minutes. Add reserved stock and bring to a boil. Reduce heat to medium-high and cook until slightly thickened, about 30 minutes. Keep soup warm.

3 Whip remaining cream in a bowl until semi-stiff peaks form; set aside. Melt remaining butter in a 12" skillet over medium-high. Season langoustine tail meat with salt and pepper and cook, flipping once, until cooked through, 3–5 minutes. Divide soup between bowls and top with langoustine meat. Garnish with whipped cream and chives.

In Japanese homes, *ozoni* is traditionally eaten on the first day of the year. It combines slices of pink-rimmed fish cake, chicken, daikon, carrot, and shiitake mushrooms in a flavorful broth. It also includes chewy rice cakes (*mochi*), which are first oven toasted until they resemble campfire marshmallows.

JAPANESE NEW YEAR SOUP

4   dried shiitake mushrooms

4   cups chicken stock

2   boneless, skinless chicken thighs, cut into 1″ pieces

4   oz. daikon radish, peeled and sliced ¼″ thick on the bias

1   carrot, sliced ¼″ thick on the bias

4   oz. kamaboko (Japanese fish cake), sliced ¼″ thick

1   cup spinach, stemmed

1   tbsp. sake

1   tsp. soy sauce

   Kosher salt, to taste

4   kiri mochi (glutinous rice cakes), 1 x 2″, about ½″ thick

   Fresh mitsuba (Japanese wild parsley) or flat-leaf parsley sprigs, to garnish

SERVES 4

1 Place shiitakes in a bowl. Bring 1 cup stock to a boil in a 4-qt. saucepan and pour over shiitakes; let sit until softened, 4–6 minutes. Using a slotted spoon, transfer shiitakes to another bowl and discard stems. Pour stock back into pan, discarding any dirt or sediment.

2 Add remaining stock and the chicken to pan and bring to a boil. Reduce heat to medium and add daikon and carrot. Cook, stirring occasionally, until chicken is cooked through, 6–8 minutes. Add reserved shiitakes, the sliced fish cake, spinach, sake, soy sauce, and salt; cook until spinach is wilted, about 2 minutes. Keep soup warm.

3 Heat oven to 425°F. Place kiri mochi directly on an oven rack and bake, turning as needed, until browned in spots and puffed, 6–8 minutes. Divide rice cakes between 4 bowls and ladle soup over top, then garnish with mitsuba sprigs. Serve hot.

For this Tunisian-Jewish one-pot meal, which is an especially popular choice for Rosh Hashanah and Passover dinners among Jewish families in North Africa, white fish fillets are braised in a thick chile-spiced tomato sauce.

SPICY TUNISIAN FISH STEW

6	4-oz. skin-on sea bass or grouper fillets
3	tbsp. fresh lemon juice
	Kosher salt and freshly ground black pepper, to taste
¼	cup extra-virgin olive oil
10	cloves garlic, coarsely chopped
3	small red Thai chiles, stemmed and coarsely chopped
1	6-oz. can tomato paste
2	cups finely chopped fresh cilantro

SERVES 4-6

Combine fish, lemon juice, salt, and pepper in a bowl and set aside. Heat oil in a 12″ skillet over medium-high. Cook garlic and chiles until soft, 1–2 minutes. Add tomato paste and cook, stirring, until slightly caramelized, about 2 minutes. Add cilantro and 1¼ cups water and bring to a boil. Reduce heat to medium and cook until liquid is slightly reduced, about 6 minutes. Add fish, skin side up, with its marinade and cook, covered, until fish is cooked through, 18–20 minutes. Spoon stew into bowls and serve.

Salmon has been a pillar of Russian cuisine for centuries. In lean times, all parts of the fish were eaten, but here the bones and the head, as well as leeks and bay leaf, are used only to flavor the broth. Fresh salmon is poached in the fragrant liquid and punctuated with small pieces of hearty carrot and potato.

RUSSIAN SALMON SOUP

¼ cup extra-virgin olive oil

½ tsp. crushed red chile flakes

8 whole black peppercorns

4 small carrots (1 chopped, 3 thinly sliced)

4 sprigs fresh dill

4 sprigs fresh flat-leaf parsley

2 bay leaves

2 leeks, white parts only, sliced ¼" thick crosswise and rinsed

2 ribs celery, coarsely chopped

1 lb. fish bones, rinsed (ask your fishmonger to do this)

1½ cups dry white wine

1 salmon head (about 1 lb.), gills removed, rinsed

3 medium Yukon gold potatoes, peeled and cut into ¼" pieces

1 lb. boneless, skinless salmon, cut into 1" pieces

1 tbsp. fresh lemon juice

Kosher salt and freshly ground black pepper, to taste

4 scallions, thinly sliced on the bias, to garnish

SERVES 6

1 Heat oil in a 6-qt. saucepan over medium-high. Cook chile flakes, peppercorns, chopped carrot, dill, parsley, bay leaves, leeks, and celery until vegetables are soft, about 10 minutes. Add fish bones, wine, salmon head, and 6 cups water and bring to a boil. Reduce heat to medium-low; cover and cook, skimming off any froth that rises to the surface, for 35 minutes. Strain the stock through a fine-mesh sieve into a bowl, and discard solids.

2 Wipe pan clean and add reserved stock. Add sliced carrots and the potatoes and bring to a boil. Reduce heat to medium-low and cook, covered, until carrots and potatoes are tender, about 25 minutes.

3 Stir in salmon and simmer just until cooked through, about 5 minutes. Gently stir in lemon juice, salt, and pepper so as not to break up the salmon. Ladle soup into bowls and garnish with scallions.

CROUTONS & CRACKERS

Different soups require different types of crackers and croutons. A brothy soup like French onion calls for a sturdy bread crouton that can soak up all the delicious liquid and remain intact. Thicker soups, like clam chowder, are best topped with a few oyster crackers at a time so that each spoonful has both cream and crunch. Fortunately, you don't have to settle for store-bought varieties. The recipes that follow are easy homemade additions for your soups and stews.

BASIC CROUTONS

- 8 oz. stale crusty Italian or French white bread, cut into 1" cubes
- 3 tbsp. extra-virgin olive oil
- 1 tbsp. finely chopped flat-leaf parsley or 2 tsp. dried parsley flakes

  Kosher salt, to taste

1 Heat oven to 375°F. Toss bread, oil, parsley, and salt on a parchment paper–lined baking sheet.

2 Bake bread cubes until golden and crisp, about 20 minutes. Set aside to cool completely. They will keep in an airtight container up to 2 weeks.

VERY THIN CROUTONS

- 6 slices Pepperidge Farm Very Thinly Sliced Enriched Bread
- 1 tbsp. unsalted butter, melted

  Kosher salt, to taste

1 Preheat oven to 300°F. Trim off crusts from bread. Cut slices into 1" x 1¼" rectangles.

2 Gently toss bread with butter and salt in a wide bowl. Spread seasoned rectangles on a baking sheet, spacing them at least ½" apart. Toast in oven, turning once, until golden brown and crisp, about 10 minutes.

3 Set croutons aside to cool completely. They will keep in an airtight container up to 2 weeks.

HARDTACK CRACKERS

- 1½ cups all-purpose flour, plus more for dusting
- ½ cup light rye flour
- ½ cup whole wheat flour
- ¼ cup sugar
- 8 tbsp. unsalted butter, cubed and chilled
- 1½ tbsp. kosher salt
- ¾ cup ice-cold water

1 Pulse flours, sugar, butter, and salt in a food processor until reduced to pea-size crumbles. With the motor running, slowly add water until dough forms. Form dough into a disk and wrap in plastic wrap. Chill 30 minutes.

2 Heat oven to 325°F. On a lightly floured work surface, roll dough ⅛" thick; trim edges to make a 21" square. Using a pastry cutter or knife, cut dough into 3" squares and transfer to parchment paper–lined baking sheets. Bake until crisp, about 40 minutes.

3 Set crackers aside to cool completely. They will keep in an airtight container up to 2 weeks.

The Garifuna are descendants of West and Central Africans who now live in Belize, Honduras, Guatemala, Nicaragua, and Puerto Rico, where they've incorporated their local seafood into this alluring stew, filled with vegetables and herbs and fragrant with coconut milk.

GARIFUNA-STYLE SEAFOOD SOUP

¼ cup canola oil

1 small green bell pepper, stemmed, seeded, and finely chopped

1 small yellow onion, finely chopped

2 tbsp. finely chopped fresh oregano

1 tbsp. finely chopped fresh sage

1½ tsp. ground cumin

4 cloves garlic, finely chopped

4 cups coconut milk

2 cups fish stock (page 216)

¼ cup packed basil leaves, thinly sliced

1 tsp. sugar

1 lb. conch meat, pounded ¼" thick and cut into 1" pieces, or 1 lb. clam meat

½ lb. squid bodies, sliced into ¼"-thick rings

1 lb. medium shrimp, peeled and deveined, tails left on

½ lb. cooked lobster meat, cut into 1" pieces

½ lb. mussels, scrubbed and debearded

Kosher salt and freshly ground black pepper, to taste

Lime wedges, for serving

SERVES 6

Heat oil in an 8-qt. saucepan over medium-high. Cook bell pepper and onion, stirring occasionally, until golden, 6–8 minutes. Add oregano, sage, cumin, and garlic and cook until fragrant, 1–2 minutes. Add coconut milk, stock, basil, and sugar and bring to a boil. Reduce heat to medium and add conch and squid; cook, covered, until conch is tender, about 8 minutes. Stir in shrimp, lobster meat, and mussels and cook, covered, until mussel shells open, 4–6 minutes more; discard any mussels that failed to open. Season soup with salt and pepper and ladle into bowls. Serve with lime wedges.

Known in northeastern Scotland as *partan bree,* this soup gains depth and complexity from a quick stock made from roasted crab shells and brandy. Unctuous cream sherry adds sweetness while white peppercorns lend a mellow heat to this luxurious bisque.

SCOTTISH CRAB BISQUE

4 lb. cooked Dungeness or blue crabs, meat removed from bodies and legs and finely chopped, shells broken into large pieces

6 tbsp. unsalted butter

2 large yellow onions (1 thinly sliced, 1 finely chopped)

½ rib celery, thinly sliced

¼ small bulb fennel, trimmed and thinly sliced

¾ cup coarsely chopped fresh flat-leaf parsley stems, plus 2 tbsp. finely chopped leaves, to garnish

1 tsp. whole white peppercorns

2 bay leaves

½ lemon, thinly sliced crosswise

2 tbsp. brandy

⅓ cup long-grain white rice

1 tbsp. tomato paste

1 tbsp. grated lemon zest

⅔ cup milk

¼ cup cream sherry

¼ cup heavy cream

2 tbsp. fresh lemon juice

½ tsp. paprika

Kosher salt and freshly ground black pepper, to taste

Crème fraîche, to garnish

SERVES 8

1 Heat oven to 400°F. Place crab shells on a baking sheet; bake until lightly browned, about 20 minutes, and set aside. Melt 4 tbsp. butter in an 8-qt. saucepan over medium-high. Add sliced onion, celery, and fennel and cook, stirring occasionally, until soft, about 5 minutes. Add reserved crab shells, parsley stems, peppercorns, bay leaves, and lemon and cook for 2 minutes. Add brandy and cook for 1 minute. Add 10 cups water and bring to a boil. Reduce heat to medium-low and cook, stirring occasionally, until slightly reduced, about 1 hour. Pour mixture through a fine-mesh sieve into a bowl and discard solids. Set crab stock aside.

2 Wipe saucepan clean, return to medium-high, and add remaining butter. Cook chopped onion until soft, 5–7 minutes. Add rice, tomato paste, and lemon zest and cook until slightly caramelized, about 2 minutes. Add reserved crab stock and bring to a boil. Reduce heat to medium-low and cook until rice is tender, about 18 minutes. Working in batches, purée soup in a blender and return to saucepan over medium. Add reserved crabmeat, milk, sherry, cream, lemon juice, paprika, salt, and pepper and cook until crab is warmed through, about 3 minutes. Divide soup between 8 bowls. Garnish each bowl with a dollop of crème fraîche and the finely chopped parsley leaves.

The trick for tender calamari, or squid, is to either barely cook it or cook it a long time. For this Sicilian stew, the primary emphasis is on building flavors in the broth, while the squid gets just a quick simmer at the end, keeping its flavor and texture intact.

SICILIAN CALAMARI & TOMATO STEW

¼ cup extra-virgin olive oil, plus more for drizzling

1 medium yellow onion, thinly sliced

1 rib celery, thinly sliced

1 small carrot, thinly sliced

1 tbsp. finely chopped fresh oregano

½ tsp. crushed red chile flakes

4 cloves garlic, thinly sliced

1 cup dry white wine

1 28-oz. can whole peeled tomatoes, crushed by hand

12 oz. squid, bodies sliced into ¼"-thick rings, tentacles kept whole

½ cup pitted cured black olives

¼ cup coarsely chopped fresh flat-leaf parsley

Kosher salt and freshly ground black pepper, to taste

Crusty bread, for serving

Lemon wedges, for serving

SERVES 4

Heat oil in a 4-qt. saucepan over medium-high. Cook onion, celery, and carrot until golden, 6–8 minutes. Add oregano, chile flakes, and garlic and cook until fragrant, 1–2 minutes. Add wine and cook, stirring occasionally, until reduced by half, 3–4 minutes. Stir in tomatoes and 2 cups water and bring to a boil. Reduce heat to medium and cook until liquid is slightly thickened, 6–8 minutes. Add squid and cook until opaque and cooked through, 3–4 minutes. Stir in olives, parsley, salt, and pepper. Ladle stew into bowls. Drizzle with oil and serve with bread and lemon wedges.

Light and tangy, with a modest amount of chile heat, this seafood and vegetable soup is a classic of central Thailand. The broth is tart and pungent but also delivers measured amounts of sweetness, salt, and spice. The curry paste calls for krachai, a milder relative of ginger.

SOUR CURRY SOUP WITH SHRIMP

FOR THE CURRY PASTE

- 30 dried red Thai chiles or chiles de árbol, stemmed and coarsely chopped
- 2 cups boiling water
- ½ lb. raw medium shrimp (about 10), peeled and deveined, tails removed, and coarsely chopped
- ¼ cup shrimp paste
- 1 tbsp. kosher salt
- 8 cloves garlic, coarsely chopped
- 6 Asian shallots or 2 regular shallots, coarsely chopped
- 1 4"-piece krachai or ginger, peeled and thinly sliced

FOR THE SOUP

- 1 cup tamarind concentrate
- 1 tbsp. fish sauce
- 1 tbsp. grated palm sugar
- ¼ lb. green beans, trimmed and cut into 2" pieces
- 1 7-oz. daikon radish, peeled, halved lengthwise, and cut into ½"-thick slices
- 1 small chayote squash, cut into 2" pieces about ½" thick
- ¼ small Napa cabbage, sliced 2" thick
- ½ lb. raw medium shrimp (about 10), peeled and deveined, tails removed

  Cooked jasmine rice, for serving

SERVES 6–8

1 Make the curry paste: Place chiles in a bowl and cover with the boiling water; let sit until softened, about 15 minutes. Drain chiles, reserving ¼ cup liquid. Place chiles in a small food processor with raw shrimp, shrimp paste, salt, garlic, shallots, and krachai and pulse until coarsely chopped. Add reserved chile liquid and purée until smooth. Set 1½ cups paste aside (refrigerate remaining paste for another use for up to 1 week).

2 Make the soup: Whisk the 1½ cups curry paste with tamarind, fish sauce, and palm sugar in a 4-qt. saucepan or 13" wok until smooth. Whisk in 4 cups water and bring to a boil. Add green beans, daikon, chayote, and cabbage and reduce heat to medium. Cook, stirring occasionally, until vegetables are tender, 20–25 minutes. Add shrimp and cook until pink and cooked through, 1–2 minutes. Remove from heat and let curry sit for 20–30 minutes for flavors to meld. Serve with jasmine rice on the side.

The quintessential dish of the Dalmatian coast is a hearty fish stew called *brodet,* often made with monkfish. Although the possibilities for what goes in a *brodet* are open to creative interpretation, the guidelines for how to cook it are not: You layer the ingredients in the pot, you put the pot on the fire, and you don't stir the contents. Less than 30 minutes later, the stew is done. This technique ensures that the fish fillets remain intact.

CROATIAN FISH STEW

1   cup fresh packed parsley leaves

½   cup extra-virgin olive oil, plus more for greasing

¼   cup fresh lemon juice

14   cloves garlic, thinly sliced

Kosher salt and freshly ground black pepper, to taste

1   lb. skinless monkfish fillets, pin bones removed

1   lb. skinless sea bass fillets, pin bones removed

10   oz. raw medium shrimp, peeled and deveined, tails removed

6   raw, unpeeled langoustines, heads on (optional)

1   lb. Yukon gold potatoes, peeled and thinly sliced

2   small leeks, white and light green parts only, halved, thinly sliced, and rinsed

1   large red onion, thinly sliced

1   large yellow onion, thinly sliced

1   cup dry white wine

1   28-oz. can whole peeled tomatoes, crushed by hand

SERVES 8

1 Purée parsley, half the oil, the lemon juice, half the garlic, salt, and pepper in a food processor until smooth; transfer to a large bowl. Add monkfish, sea bass, shrimp, and, if using, the langoustines and toss to combine. Cover with plastic wrap and chill for 10 minutes.

2 Grease an 8-qt. Dutch oven with oil. Toss remaining garlic, the potatoes, leeks, and onions in a bowl; spread ⅓ of the mixture in bottom of pot. Add ⅓ each of the remaining oil, the wine, and the tomatoes. Remove shrimp and langoustines from marinade and set aside; arrange ⅓ of the remaining fish mixture over the tomatoes. Repeat layering and add 1 cup water; cover and bring to a boil. Reduce heat to medium-low and cook, shaking pot occasionally but not stirring, until fish and vegetables are tender, 12–15 minutes. Add reserved shrimp and langoustines. Cover and cook until shellfish is pink and cooked through, about 5 minutes more. Spoon stew into bowls and serve.

It is said that the Portuguese have 365 ways to use dried salt cod, or *bacalhau*—one for each day of the year. What originated centuries ago as a means to preserve fresh fish has become a staple in Portuguese (and, as a result, Brazilian) cooking for its salty-sweet cured flavor and chewy texture. The salt cod is rinsed and rehydrated before being combined with coconut milk and dried chiles in this recipe from Brazilian food writer Neide Rigo.

BRAZILIAN SALT COD STEW

2   lb. boneless salt cod

¼   cup extra-virgin olive oil

1   tbsp. sweet paprika

6   fresh basil leaves

4   cloves garlic, finely chopped

2   dried chiles de árbol, chopped

2   plum tomatoes, peeled, cored, and quartered

1   large onion, thinly sliced

1   cup coconut milk

1   cup chopped scallions

1   cup finely chopped fresh flat-leaf parsley

Cooked white rice, for serving

SERVES 4–6

1 Put the cod into a bowl. Add cold water and soak for 15 minutes. Drain and transfer cod to a 3-qt. plastic container and cover with fresh water. Cover and refrigerate for 18–24 hours, changing water at least 3 times. Drain cod and tear into 3″ chunks.

2 Heat oil in a 4-qt. saucepan over medium-high. Add paprika, basil, garlic, chiles, tomatoes, and onion and cook, stirring, until soft, 5–8 minutes. Add cod and 1 cup water and bring to a boil. Reduce heat to medium-low and simmer, covered, until cod is flaky, 8–10 minutes. Stir in coconut milk and bring to a boil. Remove from heat and stir in scallions and parsley. Cover and let sit for 5 minutes. Serve with rice.

Every region of Thailand has its version of *kaeng khiaw,* or green curry. In this delicious and fragrant take from the country's center, Thai-style dumplings add a nice bouncy texture to the dish. Make your own or buy fresh or frozen fish balls from an Asian grocery.

GREEN CURRY WITH FISH & EGGPLANT

FOR THE CURRY PASTE

- 2 tsp. coriander seeds
- 1 tsp. yellow mustard seeds
- ½ tsp. cumin seeds
- 8 whole black peppercorns
- 2 tbsp. coarsely chopped fresh cilantro root or stems
- 2 tsp. shrimp paste
- 1½ tsp. kosher salt
- 1 tsp. finely chopped kaffir lime leaf
- 1 tsp. grated lime zest
- 15 green Thai chiles, stemmed and coarsely chopped
- 8 cloves garlic, coarsely chopped
- 6 small Asian shallots or 2 medium regular shallots, thinly sliced
- 2 stalks lemongrass, trimmed and thinly sliced
- 1 3"-piece galangal, peeled and thinly sliced
- ¼ cup coconut milk

FOR THE FISH BALLS

- ½ lb. boneless, skinless tilapia fillets, cut into ½" pieces
- ¾ tsp. kosher salt, plus more to taste
- 4 tsp. cornstarch
- ½ tsp. sugar
- ⅛ tsp. ground white pepper

FOR THE CURRY

- ½ cup coconut cream
- 1½ cups coconut milk
- 4 small Thai eggplants, quartered, or 1 small Japanese eggplant, cut into 1½" pieces
- 1 tbsp. fish sauce
- 1 tbsp. grated palm sugar
- 12 fresh or frozen kaffir lime leaves, coarsely torn
- 3–4 green Thai chiles, stemmed and halved
- ½ cup packed basil leaves, preferably Thai
- 2 hard-cooked eggs, peeled and quartered, for serving
  Cooked jasmine rice, for serving

SERVES 6–8

1 Make the curry paste: Heat coriander seeds, mustard seeds, cumin seeds, and peppercorns in a 12" cast-iron skillet until seeds begin to pop, 1–2 minutes; let cool slightly. Place in a spice grinder and pulse until finely ground, then set aside.

2 Combine cilantro root, shrimp paste, salt, lime leaf, lime zest, chiles, garlic, shallots, lemongrass, and galangal in a small food processor and pulse until coarsely chopped. Add reserved spice mixture and the coconut milk and purée until smooth. Set ½ cup aside (refrigerate remaining paste for another use for up to 2 weeks).

3 Make the fish balls: Pulse fish and salt in a food processor. With the motor running, slowly add 2 tbsp. water and process into a smooth paste. Add cornstarch, sugar, and white pepper and pulse until combined. Transfer paste to a bowl and chill for 30 minutes.

4 Bring a large pot of salted water to a boil. Using wet hands, roll fish paste into sixteen 1" balls. Cook, partially covered, until tender, 6–7 minutes. Using a slotted spoon, transfer balls to a plate and let cool completely.

5 Make the curry: Heat coconut cream in a 6-qt. saucepan or 13" wok over medium and cook, stirring occasionally, until oil is separated, 8–10 minutes. Add the ½ cup reserved curry paste and cook, stirring, until fragrant and slightly browned, about 4 minutes. Add coconut milk and 1 cup water and bring to a boil. Add fish balls and eggplant. Reduce heat to medium-low and cook, stirring occasionally, until eggplant is tender, about 20 minutes. Stir in fish sauce, palm sugar, lime leaves, and chiles. Remove from heat and stir in basil. Serve with eggs and jasmine rice on the side.

VEGETABLE

Imagine a minestrone in which the vegetables are light and bright, even a little crunchy. In Lidia Bastianich's delicious take on the Umbrian classic, the vegetables are cooked relatively briefly to preserve their market-fresh texture.

UMBRIAN VEGETABLE SOUP

½   **cup packed fresh basil leaves**

¼   **cup extra-virgin olive oil, plus more for drizzling**

2   **tbsp. finely chopped fresh flat-leaf parsley**

4   **cloves garlic**

½   **medium onion, coarsely chopped**

½   **lb. new potatoes, cut into ½″ pieces**

3   **ribs celery, finely chopped**

2   **carrots, finely chopped**

2   **plum tomatoes, finely chopped**

  Kosher salt and freshly ground black pepper, to taste

3   **oz. spinach, stemmed**

1½   **cups canned cannellini beans, drained and rinsed**

1   **cup fresh or frozen green peas**

½   **small head frisée, leaves cut into bite-size pieces**

  Grated Grana Padano or Parmigiano-Reggiano, for serving

SERVES 6-8

1 Combine half the basil, 2 tbsp. oil, the parsley, garlic, and onion in a food processor. Pulse until coarsely chopped.

2 Heat remaining oil in an 8-qt. saucepan over medium-high. Cook herb-garlic mixture, stirring occasionally, until slightly dry, about 5 minutes. Add potatoes, celery, carrots, and tomatoes and cook, stirring occasionally, until vegetables are golden brown, about 6 minutes. Season with salt and add 4 cups water; bring to a boil. Reduce heat to medium-low, cover, and cook, stirring occasionally, until vegetables are tender, about 20 minutes. Stir in spinach, beans, peas, and frisée and cook until greens are wilted and just tender, about 10 minutes. Season soup with salt and pepper, and stir in remaining basil. Ladle soup into bowls, sprinkle with Grana Padano, and drizzle with oil.

Parsley takes center stage in this bright green soup. The delicately flavored, simple purée, garnished with fiery, freshly grated horseradish, is a perfect first course.

CREAM OF PARSLEY SOUP WITH FRESH HORSERADISH

1   lb. fresh flat-leaf parsley

3   tbsp. unsalted butter

2   cloves garlic, thinly sliced

1   large yellow onion, thinly sliced

    Kosher salt and freshly ground black pepper, to taste

4   cups vegetable or chicken stock

1   cup heavy cream

    Juice of 1 lemon

    Freshly grated horseradish, for serving

SERVES 6-8

1 Bring a 6-qt. saucepan of water to a boil. Cook parsley until bright green and wilted, 30 seconds–1 minute. Using tongs, transfer parsley to a bowl of ice water and let sit for 1 minute. Drain parsley and squeeze dry completely, then coarsely chop and set aside.

2 Discard water from pan and add butter; melt over medium. Cook garlic, onion, salt, and pepper, stirring occasionally, until onion is soft, about 6 minutes. Add stock and heavy cream and bring to a simmer over medium-high. Cook, stirring occasionally, until slightly reduced, 15–20 minutes. Stir in reserved parsley, salt, and pepper and cook until warmed through, about 5 minutes. Using an immersion blender or regular blender, purée soup until smooth. Strain soup through a fine-mesh sieve, if you like, and stir in lemon juice. Ladle soup into bowls and garnish with horseradish.

LIGHTEN IT UP

Heavy cream is a luxurious addition to any soup: It adds a satisfying body and buttery richness to everything from crab bisque to clam chowder to creamy tomato soup. But this luscious indulgence comes with a high fat and calorie content.

Fortunately, there are ways to create an equally satisfying effect with less-rich ingredients, and the blender is your best friend in this endeavor. Almost every vegetable, bean, and nut can be transformed into a creamy soup that's so delicious you'll never miss the full-fat version.

Less traditional dairy products, like Greek yogurt and buttermilk, as well as coconut milk can add layers of flavor, mimicking the body and richness of cream but without as much fat. Almonds and cashews, soaked and puréed, also work for a full-bodied chilled summer soup. A vegetable soup swirled with some cannellini beans and sieved through cheesecloth turns into a velvety purée. With a light drizzle of extra-virgin olive oil, it is ready for company.

The simple act of charring and puréeing eggplant flesh results in a deeply flavored, smoky base that's incredibly silky. Add a finishing dollop of tzatziki for a cold, crisp contrast.

CHARRED EGGPLANT SOUP WITH TZATZIKI

FOR THE SOUP

- 4 large eggplants, halved lengthwise
- 8 cloves garlic, smashed
- 6 tbsp. tahini
- 2 tsp. Aleppo pepper or paprika, plus more to garnish

   Grated zest and juice of 1 lemon
- 4 cups vegetable stock
- 2 cups plain, full-fat Greek yogurt

   Kosher salt and freshly ground black pepper, to taste

FOR THE TZATZIKI & GARNISH

- ¼ cup plain, full-fat Greek yogurt
- 1 tbsp. finely chopped fresh mint, plus thinly sliced leaves to garnish
- 1 tbsp. fresh lemon juice
- 2 tsp. finely chopped fresh dill
- 1 clove garlic, mashed into a paste
- ½ small English cucumber, coarsely grated and squeezed dry
- ½ small shallot, finely chopped

   Kosher salt and freshly ground black pepper, to taste

   Extra-virgin olive oil, to garnish

   Grilled pita bread, for serving

1 Make the soup: Heat oven broiler. Place eggplant cut side down on a baking sheet and prick all over with a knife. Broil, flipping once, until skin is charred and eggplant is tender, 15 minutes. Let eggplant cool, then peel and transfer to a blender along with the garlic. Add tahini, Aleppo pepper, lemon zest and juice, 2 cups stock, the yogurt, salt, and pepper; purée until smooth and transfer to a 4-qt. saucepan. Add remaining stock and bring to a simmer over medium-high. Cook until soup is warmed through and thickened, 4–6 minutes.

2 Meanwhile, make the tzatziki and garnish: Combine yogurt, mint, lemon juice, dill, garlic paste, cucumber, shallot, salt, and pepper in a bowl. Ladle soup into bowls and garnish with a dollop of tzatziki. Drizzle with oil and sprinkle with Aleppo pepper and sliced mint. Serve with grilled pita bread.

SERVES 6

Forget butternut squash. This soup, which highlights the best of autumn produce, should be your new go-to for the fall season. A dash of vinegar perks up the slightly sweet base, and a finishing swirl of crème fraîche adds tang and richness.

PEAR, SHALLOT & DELICATA SQUASH SOUP

2   tbsp. extra-virgin olive oil

4   shallots, thinly sliced

1   lb. delicata squash, peeled, seeded, and cut into ½" slices (about 2 cups)

1   lb. ripe firm-fleshed pears, such as Bartlett or Anjou, peeled, cored, and cut into ½" pieces

½   tsp. dried thyme

4   cups vegetable or chicken stock

1   tbsp. balsamic vinegar

Kosher salt and freshly ground black pepper, to taste

Crème fraîche, to garnish

Maple syrup, to garnish

SERVES 6-8

Heat oil in a 6-qt. saucepan over medium. Cook shallots, stirring occasionally, until golden, 4–5 minutes. Add squash and pears and cook, stirring occasionally, until squash is just tender, about 7 minutes. Stir in thyme and cook until fragrant, about 1 minute. Add stock and simmer until squash is mushy, 15–20 minutes more. Stir in vinegar, salt, and pepper. Using an immersion blender or regular blender, purée soup until smooth and ladle into bowls. Garnish with a swirl of crème fraîche and a drizzle of maple syrup.

THE IMMERSION BLENDER

An immersion blender, when used properly, is great for making soup with a more rustic texture. Because the blade is small and is constantly moved throughout the mixture, the ingredients get puréed less thoroughly, ideal for a hearty soup like bean and kale or winter squash. Remember to take the pot off the heat before blending—sticking a blender into bubbling soup is a great way to ruin the blender, and your clothes.

The secret to the intense flavor of this delicious tomato soup is to smoke the plum tomatoes in a stove-top smoker before you cook them down in red wine. Toasted baguette slices spread with garlic butter are the perfect accompaniment.

SMOKED TOMATO SOUP

2 tbsp. mesquite wood chips for an indoor smoker

3 lb. ripe plum tomatoes, halved

⅓ cup extra-virgin olive oil

10 cloves garlic, finely chopped

1 medium yellow onion, thinly sliced

1 cup dry red wine

2 cups vegetable or chicken stock

Kosher salt and freshly ground black pepper, to taste

¼ cup coarsely chopped fresh sage

¼ cup coarsely chopped fresh tarragon

2 tbsp. sherry vinegar

12 oz. baguette, thinly sliced on the bias

½ cup unsalted butter, softened

Microflowers, to garnish (optional)

Crème fraîche, to garnish

SERVES 6-8

1 Prepare a stove-top smoker: Place wood chips in a small pile in center of smoker bottom. Place drip tray and rack on top of wood chips. Arrange tomatoes on rack, cut side down, and slide on lid. Place smoker on a stove-top burner over medium. When smoke appears, let tomatoes smoke for about 7 minutes. Turn off heat and let sit, covered, for 10 minutes.

2 Heat oil in a 4-qt. saucepan over medium-high. Cook half the garlic and the onion until soft, 5–7 minutes. Add wine and bring to a boil. Cook until reduced by half, 5–7 minutes. Add smoked tomatoes, stock, salt, and pepper and return to a boil. Reduce heat to medium and cook until tomatoes break down and soup is slightly thick, 45–60 minutes. Stir in sage, tarragon, and vinegar. Working in batches, purée soup in a blender until smooth. Return to saucepan and keep warm.

3 Heat oven to 350°F. Place baguette slices in a single layer on a baking sheet and toast until lightly browned, 8–10 minutes. Mix remaining garlic, the butter, salt, and pepper in a bowl; spread butter on baguette slices and sprinkle with microflowers. Ladle soup into bowls and garnish with a swirl of crème fraîche.

At restaurants in Mexico City, chefs outdo one another with stylish soups like this silken broth of puréed pan-toasted chiles, tomatoes, and onion. Each bowl is topped with a quartet of colorful, flavorful garnishes: crisp-fried tortilla strips, julienned *pasilla* chile, cooling *crema,* and thinly sliced avocado.

ANCHO CHILE SOUP WITH AVOCADO, CREMA & PASILLA CHILES

3   dried ancho chiles
    Boiling water, as needed
4   medium plum tomatoes, cored
2   cloves garlic
1   small white onion, halved
½   cup canola oil
8   small dried pasilla chiles
8   cups vegetable
    or chicken stock
    Kosher salt and freshly
    ground black pepper,
    to taste
½   lb. queso fresco, crumbled
8   sprigs fresh cilantro,
    finely chopped, plus more
    to garnish
½   cup crema or sour cream
1   avocado, pitted, peeled,
    and thinly sliced
    Fried tortilla strips,
    to garnish

SERVES 6-8

1 Heat a 6-qt. Dutch oven over medium-high. Cook ancho chiles, flipping once, until lightly toasted, about 5 minutes. Transfer chiles to a bowl and add boiling water to cover; let sit until softened, about 30 minutes. Drain chiles, reserving soaking liquid; discard stems and seeds. Transfer chiles to a blender and set aside. Return pot to medium-high and add tomatoes, garlic, and onion. Cook, turning as needed, until blackened all over, about 10 minutes. Transfer to blender and purée with chile until smooth. Pour through a fine-mesh sieve into a bowl, and set chile purée aside.

2 Return pot to medium-high and add ¼ cup oil. Fry pasilla chiles, flipping once, until crisp, about 5 minutes. Transfer chiles to paper towels to drain. Discard oil and wipe pan clean.

3 Return pot to medium-high and add remaining oil. Fry reserved chile purée, stirring constantly, until slightly reduced, about 6 minutes. Add stock, salt, and pepper; bring to a boil and remove from heat. Divide queso fresco and cilantro between bowls and ladle soup over. Garnish with cilantro, a dollop of crema, sliced avocado, tortilla strips, and the reserved fried pasilla chiles.

Egg drop soup is a comforting and simple staple to have in your soup repertoire. Here it's enlivened with cooked edamame and spinach leaves, but you can feel free to add almost any vegetable. Just make sure it's precooked, like the edamame here, or a quick-cooking choice, like the spinach.

SPINACH & EDAMAME EGG DROP SOUP

6	cups vegetable or chicken stock
1½	tsp. kosher salt, plus more to taste
1	1" piece ginger, peeled and finely grated
1½	tbsp. cornstarch
1	tbsp. soy sauce
1	tbsp. toasted sesame oil
3	eggs
2	oz. baby spinach
1½	cups cooked, shelled edamame
4	scallions, thinly sliced, to garnish

SERVES 4

1 Combine stock, 1 tsp. salt, and ginger in a 4-qt. saucepan and bring to a boil. Whisk cornstarch and soy sauce in a bowl until smooth and whisk into stock. Cook until broth is slightly thickened, 1–2 minutes, and remove from heat.

2 Whisk remaining salt, the sesame oil, and eggs in a bowl. Slowly add egg mixture to pan while gently whisking broth to scatter eggs as they cook. Stir in spinach and edamame and season with salt. Ladle soup into bowls and garnish with scallions.

A garnish of fried shiitake mushrooms and a drizzle of spiced mint butter add elegance to this fragrant soup, which makes the most of the cool-weather harvest.

ACORN SQUASH & APPLE SOUP

2 tbsp. extra-virgin olive oil

1 large yellow onion, finely chopped

1 tsp. ground turmeric

½ tsp. Chinese five-spice powder

2 cloves garlic, finely chopped

1 1″ piece ginger, peeled and finely chopped

1¾ lb. acorn squash, peeled, seeded, and cut into ½″ pieces

4 cups vegetable stock

2 tart apples, such as Granny Smith, peeled, cored, and cut into ½″ pieces

Kosher salt and freshly ground black pepper, to taste

1 tbsp. fresh lime juice

1 cup canola oil

1 cup thinly sliced stemmed shiitake mushrooms

6 tbsp. unsalted butter

1 tsp. dried mint

½ tsp. ground cumin

½ tsp. paprika

SERVES 6–8

1 Heat olive oil in a 6-qt. saucepan over medium-high. Cook onion, stirring occasionally, until golden, about 15 minutes. Stir in turmeric, five-spice powder, garlic, and ginger and cook until fragrant, about 1 minute. Add squash, stock, apples, salt, and pepper and bring to a boil. Cover and cook, stirring occasionally, until squash and apple are tender, about 15 minutes. Transfer soup to a blender and purée until smooth. Stir in the lime juice and keep warm.

2 Heat canola oil in a 2-qt. saucepan over medium-high until a deep-fry thermometer reads 350°F. Fry mushrooms until browned and crisp, about 3 minutes. Using a slotted spoon, transfer mushrooms to paper towels to drain; set aside and reserve oil for another use. Wipe pan clean and add butter, mint, cumin, paprika, salt, and pepper; heat over medium and cook, stirring, until melted and fragrant, about 5 minutes. Ladle soup into bowls. Drizzle with spiced mint butter and garnish with fried mushrooms.

Both fennel and Pernod taste of anise, but the vegetable does so in a more subtle way, the liqueur in a more bracing one. Put them together, as in this creamy soup, and the result is a dish with delicious complexity.

CREAM OF FENNEL SOUP

1 tsp. coriander seeds

2 green cardamom pods, crushed

2 star anise

1 whole clove

¼ cup canola oil

5 lb. fennel bulbs, trimmed and coarsely chopped

1 large leek, white and light green parts only, coarsely chopped and rinsed

1 large yellow onion, coarsely chopped

1 cup dry white wine

6 cups vegetable or chicken stock

½ cup heavy cream

¼ cup Pernod

Kosher salt and freshly ground white pepper, to taste

Minced chives, to garnish

Crusty bread, for serving (optional)

SERVES 6-8

1 Heat coriander, cardamom, star anise, and clove in an 8-qt. saucepan over medium-high. Cook until seeds begin to pop, 2–3 minutes. Transfer spices to a piece of cheesecloth and tie into a tight bundle. Set aside.

2 Add oil to pan and return to medium-high. Cook fennel, leek, and onion, stirring occasionally, until golden, 25–30 minutes. Add wine and cook until reduced by half, 3–4 minutes. Add reserved spice bundle and the stock and bring to a boil. Reduce heat to medium-low and cook, stirring occasionally, until vegetables are very tender, about 10 minutes. Discard spice bundle and, working in batches, purée soup in a blender until smooth. Return soup to saucepan; add cream, Pernod, salt, and white pepper, and bring to a simmer. Cook soup until slightly thickened, 3–5 minutes. Ladle into bowls, garnish with chives, and serve with crusty bread.

In this riff on a popular German-by-way-of-Wisconsin soup, the traditional cheddar is cut through with piquant Gorgonzola for a zesty, luxurious finish. A slice of crusty bread on the side, and that's all you'll need to get through a cold winter's night.

BEER CHEESE SOUP

2   tbsp. unsalted butter

3   large shallots, finely chopped

1   medium carrot,
      coarsely shredded

1   medium onion, finely chopped

⅓   cup flour

1¾   cups vegetable stock

1   cup milk

1   tsp. caraway seeds, crushed

      Kosher salt and freshly
      ground black pepper, to taste

10   oz. shredded sharp
      cheddar cheese

6   oz. beer, preferably ale

      Crumbled Gorgonzola cheese,
      to garnish

      Crusty bread, for serving
      (optional)

SERVES 4

Melt butter in a 4-qt. saucepan over medium-high. Cook shallots, carrot, and onion until soft, 4–6 minutes. Stir in flour and cook for 2 minutes more. Add stock, milk, caraway seeds, salt, and pepper and simmer until soup is thickened, 8–10 minutes. Add cheddar and beer and cook until cheese is melted, 2–3 minutes. Ladle soup into bowls and top with Gorgonzola. Serve with crusty bread.

This soup highlights the best of mushrooms by using them in three distinct forms. A mix of fresh mushrooms is simmered in stock and puréed along with rehydrated dried porcinis to form an umami-packed base. To finish, panfried mushrooms add satisfying texture.

CREAM OF ROASTED MUSHROOM SOUP

1   oz. dried porcini mushrooms

2   cups boiling water

2   lb. mixed fresh mushrooms, such as cremini, oyster, shiitake, and white button (1½ lb. halved, 8 oz. thinly sliced)

⅓   cup extra-virgin olive oil

1½   tbsp. fresh thyme leaves

5   cloves garlic, crushed

1   small yellow onion, thinly sliced

Kosher salt and freshly ground black pepper, to taste

5   cups vegetable or chicken stock

3   tbsp. unsalted butter

1   cup heavy cream

1½   tbsp. sherry

¼   tsp. freshly grated nutmeg

Crème fraîche, to garnish

Finely chopped chives, to garnish

SERVES 4-6

1 Combine porcini and boiling water in a bowl and let sit until softened, about 30 minutes. Using a slotted spoon, transfer mushrooms to a blender along with 1½ cups soaking liquid, discarding any dirt or sediment; set aside.

2 Heat oven to 450°F. Toss halved mixed mushrooms, the oil, thyme, garlic, onion, salt, and pepper on a baking sheet; roast, stirring occasionally, until golden brown, 15–20 minutes. Transfer mushroom mixture to a blender, add 1 cup stock, and purée until smooth; set purée aside.

3 Melt butter in a 4-qt. saucepan over medium-high. Cook sliced mushrooms until golden, 6–8 minutes. Add reserved mushroom purée and remaining stock and bring to a boil. Reduce heat to medium and stir in cream, sherry, nutmeg, salt, and pepper. Cook soup, stirring occasionally, until slightly thickened, about 25 minutes. Ladle into bowls and garnish with a dollop of crème fraîche and a sprinkling of chives.

HOW TO BOOST UMAMI

The term *umami* refers to the subtle "fifth taste" (after sweet, sour, salty, and bitter) experienced when eating foods like cured meats, mushrooms, and many aged cheeses. It's generally believed the unique flavor comes mainly from three naturally occurring compounds: the amino acid ion glutamate and the two compounds inosinate and guanylate, all of which exist in various concentrations in our favorite umami-rich foods. To add a complex, highly savory boost to your soups and stews, try any of these umami-packed ingredients.

PARMESAN CHEESE Toss a hunk of parmesan, including the rind, into your meat or vegetable stock as it simmers for a foolproof flavor transformation.

KOMBU This dried seaweed provides a complex salinity when steeped (not simmered) in water. Use the water as a savory base for making stock.

DRIED MUSHROOMS Like *kombu*, dried porcini or shiitakes can be soaked and their liquid used for a soup base. Cook the liquid down until reduced by half and use in place of a vegetable broth.

TOMATOES Naturally high in glutamate, ripe tomatoes are perhaps the easiest umami booster and can lend character and depth, along with sweetness and acidity, to an otherwise simple soup.

SPRINKLED GARNISHES

Let your imagination run wild when it comes to choosing a sprinkled topping to finish a soup or stew. Sliced or chopped nuts, crispy noodles, tortilla chips, fried bacon, and prosciutto bits add texture and crunch along with depth of flavor. Shredded or grated cheeses will melt into the soup to contribute a creamy element. Croutons can be garlicky hunks of sturdy bread to show off a bold soup or small and delicate *pain de mie* crumbs for a refined soup, such as crab or lobster bisque. Here's a trio of recipes to get you started.

CHILE-LIME PEPITAS

These crunchy, spicy pepitas, or pumpkin seeds, give off a hit of heat and are a great addition to most vegetable-based or Mexican soups and stews.

- 1   **cup pepitas**
- 1   **tbsp. fresh lime juice**
- 1   **tsp. cayenne pepper**
      Kosher salt, to taste

MAKES 1 CUP

Heat a 10" skillet over medium; cook pepitas until toasted, 4 minutes. Add lime juice, cayenne, and salt and toss to coat. The pepitas will be a bit wet from the lime juice; spread on a baking sheet lined with paper towels to dry, tossing once or twice, about 1 hour. Store in an airtight tin or jar in a cool, dry location for up to 1 week.

GREMOLATA

You need only three ingredients to make this tangy Italian garnish, which can brighten up a variety of soups hearty enough to stand up to the garlic.

- **Grated zest from 1 lemon**
- ½   **cup finely chopped fresh flat-leaf parsley**
- 4   **cloves garlic, finely chopped**

MAKES ¼ CUP

Place lemon zest in a bowl and add parsley and garlic. Toss to mix well. Store in an airtight tin or jar in the refrigerator for up to 1 week.

FRIED GARLIC-THYME ALMONDS

You can change up the nut and herb choice for this simple and delicious topping. Walnuts, hazelnuts, rosemary, and dill are all good choices.

- 1   **tbsp. canola oil**
- 2   **cloves garlic, thinly sliced**
- 1   **cup sliced almonds**
- 2   **tbsp. dried chopped thyme**
      Kosher salt, to taste

MAKES 1 CUP

Heat oil in a 10" skillet over medium; add garlic and cook until lightly golden, 2 minutes. Add almonds and cook until nuts are toasted and garlic is crisp, 3 minutes more. Add thyme and salt and toss to coat. Remove to a baking sheet lined with paper towels and spread the nuts in a single layer until they cool to room temperature, tossing once or twice, about 40 minutes. Store in an airtight tin or jar in a cool, dry location for up to 3 weeks.

Here, a normally sweet squash soup base gets an underlying thrum of heat from Scotch bonnet pepper, which grows widely on Caribbean islands. If you prefer a more pronounced kick, don't remove all of the pepper's seeds; that's where it packs most of its punch.

CARIBBEAN WINTER SQUASH SOUP

3 tbsp. unsalted butter

4 cloves garlic, finely chopped

1 medium white onion, finely chopped

1 Scotch bonnet pepper, stemmed, seeded, and finely chopped

3 lb. winter squash, such as calabaza or butternut, peeled, seeded, and cut into ½" pieces

4 cups vegetable or chicken stock

4 sprigs fresh thyme

2 sprigs fresh flat-leaf parsley

1 bay leaf

1 cup milk

¼ cup heavy cream

½ tbsp. mild curry powder

1 tsp. fresh lime juice

¼ tsp. freshly grated nutmeg

Kosher salt and freshly ground black pepper, to taste

Crème fraîche, to garnish

SERVES 6

1 Melt butter in a 6-qt. saucepan over medium-high. Add garlic, onion, and Scotch bonnet pepper and cook until golden, about 8 minutes. Add squash, stock, thyme, parsley, and bay leaf and bring to a boil. Reduce heat to medium and cook until squash is very tender, 30–35 minutes. Discard thyme, parsley, and bay leaf.

2 Transfer soup to a blender and purée until smooth. Return soup to saucepan and stir in milk, cream, curry powder, lime juice, nutmeg, salt, and pepper; simmer until soup is slightly thickened, 4–6 minutes. Ladle soup into bowls and garnish with a swirl of crème fraîche.

When shopping for fresh peas—variously labeled green peas, English peas, shell peas, or garden peas—look for pods that are smooth and bright green and snap crisply when you bend them. Peas begin showing up in market bins in the spring and are at their best from late spring into early summer. One pound of unshelled peas yields about one cup shelled.

FRESH PEA SOUP

6   cups chicken stock

3   russet potatoes, peeled and roughly chopped

6   scallions, white part only, roughly chopped

4   cups fresh shelled peas

Kosher salt and freshly ground white pepper, to taste

Finely chopped chives, to garnish

SERVES 4

1 Bring stock to a simmer in a 6-qt. saucepan over medium-high. Reduce heat to medium-low and add potatoes; cook until tender, about 10 minutes. Add scallions and cook for 5 minutes. Increase heat to medium and add peas; cook until just tender, 3–5 minutes.

2 Transfer soup to a blender and purée until smooth. Strain soup through a fine-mesh sieve and return to pan. Season with salt and pepper and ladle into bowls. Garnish with chives.

Rasam powder—a toasted blend of dal, chiles, and whole spices—combines with curry leaves and a host of other spices in this peppery south Indian soup. It's a staple of the January harvest festival in Tamil Nadu known as Thai Pongal. Tamarind, also known as Indian date, contributes a sweet-and-sour flavor that pairs well with the aromatic seasonings.

SPICY TAMARIND SOUP

2   tbsp. toor dal (yellow pigeon peas), rinsed, soaked for 30 minutes, and drained

½   tsp. ground turmeric

6   plum tomatoes, chopped

    Kosher salt, to taste

2   tsp. rasam powder

2   tsp. tamarind paste

1   tsp. ground black pepper

1   tsp. ground coriander

1   tsp. ground cumin

½   tsp. red chile powder, such as cayenne

2   tbsp. canola oil

¼   tsp. black mustard seeds

¼   tsp. cumin seeds

¼   tsp. fenugreek seeds

15 fresh or frozen curry leaves

2   dried chiles de árbol, stemmed

2   cloves garlic, finely chopped

SERVES 4

1 Bring dal, turmeric, tomatoes, salt, and 5 cups water to a boil in a 4-qt. saucepan. Reduce heat to medium-low and cook until dal is mushy, about 45 minutes. Stir in rasam powder, tamarind paste, pepper, coriander, cumin, and chile powder and cook 5 minutes more.

2 Heat oil in an 8″ skillet over medium-high. Cook mustard, cumin, and fenugreek seeds, curry leaves, and chiles de árbol until seeds pop, 1–2 minutes. Add garlic and cook until golden, 2–3 minutes. Stir mixture into soup and serve.

BEANS
& LEGUMES

Here, ruffle-leaved, slightly bitter escarole is simmered with slices of salty Pecorino Romano until the escarole is tender, then the remaining ingredients are stirred in. The cheese provides a nutty counterpoint to the spicy sausage and creamy beans.

ESCAROLE, SAUSAGE & CANNELLINI BEAN STEW

2   tbsp. extra-virgin olive oil

1⅓   lb. hot Italian sausage links, cut into 2″ pieces

2   cloves garlic, coarsely chopped

3   15-oz. cans cannellini beans, drained with liquid reserved from 1 can

¼   cup coarsely chopped fresh flat-leaf parsley

Pinch crushed red chile flakes

Kosher salt and freshly ground black pepper, to taste

6   cups chicken stock

2   lb. escarole, thinly sliced

1   4-oz. piece Pecorino Romano (half thinly sliced, half finely grated)

SERVES 6–8

1 Heat oil in an 8-qt. saucepan over medium-high. Cook sausage, turning as needed, until browned, 12–15 minutes. Using a slotted spoon, transfer sausage to a bowl and set aside. Reduce heat to medium-low and add garlic; cook until fragrant, about 30 seconds. Add beans and reserved liquid; bring to a simmer and cook for 5 minutes. Add reserved sausage, the parsley, chile flakes, salt, and pepper and simmer for 5 minutes more. Transfer sausage mixture to a bowl and set aside.

2 Add stock to pan and bring to a boil. Add escarole and sliced Pecorino; reduce heat to medium-low and cook until escarole is wilted, 4–5 minutes. Stir in reserved sausage mixture and cook, partially covered, until soup is thickened, about 1 hour. Ladle soup into bowls and garnish with grated Pecorino.

This take on a Tuscan winter greens soup gets an unexpected flavor boost from a kitchen staple of the American South: smoked ham hock. After imparting its savory smoke to the beans, the tender meat from the hock is shredded and panfried for a crisp, flavorful topping.

WHITE BEAN & LACINATO KALE SOUP WITH SMOKED HAM HOCK

½ cup extra-virgin olive oil

3 cloves garlic, smashed

2 ribs celery, coarsely chopped

1 carrot, coarsely chopped

1 large yellow onion, coarsely chopped

8 cups chicken stock

2½ cups dried cannellini or Great Northern beans, soaked overnight and drained

1 bouquet garni (1 tsp. whole black peppercorns, 2 bay leaves, 2 sprigs fresh rosemary, and 2 sprigs fresh thyme tied in cheesecloth)

1 smoked ham hock

Kosher salt and freshly ground black pepper, to taste

4 stalks lacinato kale (cavolo nero), or other kale, stems thinly sliced, leaves halved lengthwise and thinly sliced

SERVES 8

1 Heat ¼ cup oil in an 8-qt. saucepan over medium-high. Cook garlic, celery, carrot, and onion until golden, 10–12 minutes. Add stock, beans, bouquet garni, and ham hock and bring to a boil. Reduce heat to medium and simmer, partially covered, until beans are very tender, 1–1½ hours. Discard bouquet garni. Transfer ham hock to a plate and let cool, then discard skin and bone and shred meat; set aside. Transfer half the beans to a bowl and set aside. Using an immersion blender or regular blender, purée soup until smooth. Stir in reserved beans, salt, and pepper and keep warm.

2 Heat 2 tbsp. oil in a 12″ skillet over medium-high and cook kale stems until tender, 3–4 minutes. Add kale leaves, salt, and pepper; cook until leaves are wilted, 2–3 minutes. Stir kale stems and leaves into soup. Add remaining oil to skillet and cook reserved shredded ham until crisp, 6–8 minutes. Ladle soup into bowls and top with crispy ham.

SOAKING BEANS 101

Cooking with dried beans is economical, nutritious, and delicious. With very little planning, you can have beans at the ready whenever you desire. Once you've picked over the beans for small stones and given them an initial rinse, here are the two methods for cooking them. They both yield the same results; the first is simply faster.

THE HOT SOAK

1 Place beans in a large pot and add water to cover by several inches.

2 Bring to a boil, cook for 2 or 3 minutes, then turn off the heat, cover the pot, and let beans soak for at least 4 hours.

3 Drain beans and either discard the soaking water or keep it to use as a base for soup.

4 Rinse beans with cold water and use.

TRADITIONAL METHOD

1 Place beans in a pot and cover with cold water.

2 Soak beans overnight or for at least 8 hours.

3 Drain beans, rinse with cold water, and use.

Instead of smoky ham, this embellished version of the humble New England standard features salami for an extra dose of pepperiness. The acidic, crunchy pop of whole-grain mustard contrasts nicely with the soup's creamy whisked base.

SPLIT PEA SOUP WITH SALAMI & WHOLE-GRAIN MUSTARD

2   tbsp. extra-virgin olive oil

1   3-oz. piece hard salami, cut into ¼″ pieces

1   carrot, cut into ¼″ pieces

1   rib celery, cut into ¼″ pieces

1   small yellow onion, cut into ¼″ pieces

1   tsp. finely chopped fresh rosemary

1   tsp. finely chopped fresh thyme, plus more to garnish

3   cloves garlic, finely chopped

1   bay leaf

1   lb. dried split peas

8   cups chicken stock

Kosher salt and freshly ground black pepper, to taste

Whole-grain mustard, for serving

SERVES 6-8

Heat oil in a 6-qt. saucepan over medium-high. Cook salami until fat is rendered and salami is crisp, 2–3 minutes. Using a slotted spoon, transfer salami to a bowl and set aside. Add carrot, celery, and onion to pan and cook, stirring occasionally, until golden, 6–8 minutes. Add rosemary, thyme, garlic, and bay leaf and cook until fragrant, 1–2 minutes. Stir in split peas and stock and bring to a boil. Reduce heat to medium and cook, partially covered, until peas are mushy, about 1 hour. Season with salt and pepper and using a whisk, beat peas until soup is thickened. Ladle soup into bowls and garnish with reserved salami, a dollop of whole-grain mustard, and a sprinkling of thyme.

GLOSSARY OF DRIED BEANS

Members of the legume family, beans are one of the oldest, most widespread, and most versatile staples of global cuisine. Most of the beans we consume today are either Old World species, like favas or chickpeas, or subspecies of the New World common bean (*Phaseolus vulgaris*), like kidney or black beans. Here are ten commonly used beans and some of the ways they are prepared.

BLACK BEANS Also known as turtle beans, these shiny, dark legumes are a staple of Latin American cooking. Their bold flavor is well suited to stewing with meats and spices, such as in the Brazilian national dish *feijoada*.

BLACK-EYED PEAS Also called cowpeas or southern peas, these small two-toned beans are a staple of African cooking and of the cuisine of the American South, where they are often stewed with a ham hock.

CANNELLINI BEANS These white kidney-shaped beans are larger and fluffier than the white navy or Great Northern bean. They are especially popular in Italy, where they pair well with pasta.

CHICKPEAS Also known as garbanzo beans, these round, meaty beans, which call for long, slow cooking, are popular nearly everywhere, from Spain, where they are used in *cocido madrileño*, and India, where they simmer in curries, to the Middle East, where they are made into hummus.

CRANBERRY BEANS Also known as borlotti, and a close cousin of the kidney bean, cranberries get their name from the maroon streaks on their exterior. Their mild, nutty flavor makes them a good choice for a wide variety of soups and stews, but they are equally delicious simply boiled and seasoned with olive oil, herbs, and garlic.

FAVA BEANS A favorite of both the ancient Romans and the fictional Hannibal Lecter, fava beans have a robust taste and rich texture. In parts of Latin America and Asia, they are fried and salted or spiced and sold as a street-food snack. In Egypt, they are stewed until tender and mixed with olive oil, parsley, garlic, and other seasonings to make *ful medames*, a popular breakfast dish.

NAVY BEANS This small, white, sturdy workhorse is the traditional choice for Boston baked beans. It is also a good bean to use when French *cassoulet* is on the menu.

PIGEON PEAS Also known as gandule beans or no-eyed peas, or toor dal for the yellow ones, small, sweet pigeon peas are a staple of the Caribbean kitchen, where they are often cooked with rice and spices. They are also commonly found in pantries from Asia to Africa to Latin America.

PINTO BEANS Named for their speckled skin (*pinto* is Spanish for "painted"), pinto beans can be used in chili and are the most popular choice for Mexican refried beans.

RED BEANS The term *red bean* is used for both dark red kidney beans and a smaller, rounder red bean. Kidney beans have a robust structure that allows them to absorb the flavors of whatever they are cooked with and still maintain their shape, making them a popular base for chili. The smaller red beans are more delicate and milder flavored and are used for bean and rice dishes in both the Caribbean and the American South.

Even though this simple bean stew is typical of Corsica's flavorful, unpretentious fare, it benefits from the luxury of dried porcini mushrooms. You will need just a few of them, as their deep earthiness comes through even if only a small amount is used.

CORSICAN WHITE BEAN STEW WITH DRIED MUSHROOMS

½ oz. dried porcini mushrooms

4 cups boiling water

2 tbsp. extra-virgin olive oil

4 cloves garlic, finely chopped

1 large yellow onion, finely chopped

¼ cup tomato paste

1½ cups dried cannellini beans, soaked overnight and drained

2 cups vegetable stock

2 bay leaves

1 15-oz. can whole peeled tomatoes, crushed by hand

Kosher salt and freshly ground black pepper, to taste

SERVES 6-8

1 Combine porcini and boiling water in a bowl and let sit until softened, 20–30 minutes. Using a slotted spoon, transfer mushrooms to a cutting board and finely chop. Slowly pour soaking liquid into a measuring cup until you have 3 cups, making sure to leave any sediment in bottom of bowl; discard sediment. Set mushrooms and soaking liquid aside.

2 Heat oil in a 4-qt. Dutch oven over medium-high. Cook garlic and onion until soft, about 6 minutes. Add tomato paste and cook until slightly caramelized, about 2 minutes. Add reserved mushrooms and soaking liquid, the beans, stock, bay leaves, and tomatoes and bring to a boil. Reduce heat to medium-low, partially cover, and cook, stirring occasionally, until beans are tender, 1–1½ hours. Season with salt and pepper and serve.

During a visit to the southern Indian city of Hyderabad, renowned cookbook author Madhur Jaffrey enjoyed a version of dal—a creamy, soupy blend of simmered legumes—seasoned just before serving with *tarka,* a combination of fried spices and aromatics. Jaffrey's take on the dish melds tamarind and curry leaves in the dal and mixes together toasted mustard and cumin seeds, along with chiles and whole golden garlic cloves, in the punchy garnish.

HYDERABADI-STYLE DAL

1   cup toor dal (yellow pigeon peas), rinsed, soaked for 30 minutes, and drained

¼   tsp. ground turmeric

3   tbsp. coarsely chopped fresh cilantro

1   tsp. tamarind paste

¼   tsp. red chile powder, such as cayenne

12   fresh or frozen curry leaves

7   cloves garlic (1 mashed into a paste, 6 whole)

2   plum tomatoes, peeled and finely chopped

2   small green Thai chiles or 1 serrano, stemmed and thinly sliced

1   ½″ piece ginger, peeled and grated

    Kosher salt, to taste

3   tbsp. canola oil

½   tsp. cumin seeds

¼   tsp. brown mustard seeds

3   dried chiles de árbol

SERVES 4

1 Bring dal and 8 cups water to a boil in a 6-qt. saucepan. Reduce heat to medium, stir in turmeric, and cook until dal is mushy, about 45 minutes. Stir in cilantro, tamarind paste, chile powder, curry leaves, garlic paste, tomatoes, sliced chiles, ginger, and salt and return to a boil. Reduce heat to medium and cook until slightly thickened, about 15 minutes.

2 Heat oil in an 8″ skillet over medium-high. Cook cumin and mustard seeds until they pop, 1–2 minutes. Add whole garlic cloves and the chiles de árbol. Cook until garlic is golden, 6–8 minutes, and stir into stew.

Despite its roots in rustic peasant fare, gruel is having a fashionable moment. This hearty dish is bolstered with young turnips, some roasted with the mushrooms and others sliced and used raw as a garnish. Turnip greens are repurposed into a tangy salsa for topping.

CRACKED-WHEAT PORRIDGE WITH MUSHROOMS & TURNIP-TOP SALSA

FOR THE PORRIDGE

- 1 lb. hen of the woods (maitake) mushrooms, roughly chopped
- ½ lb. small white turnips with green tops (half quartered, half thinly sliced using a mandoline, and greens chopped for salsa)
- ¼ cup extra-virgin olive oil
- 3 cloves garlic, unpeeled
  Kosher salt and freshly ground black pepper, to taste
- 1 small yellow onion, finely chopped
- 1⅔ cups cracked wheat
- ⅓ cup white wine
- 7 cups Roasted Mushroom Stock (page 217) or vegetable stock
- 2 tbsp. unsalted butter
- 1 cup grated Pecorino Romano

FOR THE SALSA

- 2 tsp. red wine vinegar
- 1½ tsp. fresh thyme leaves
- ¼ tsp. crushed red chile flakes
- 1 large shallot, finely chopped
  Kosher salt, to taste
- ¼ cup finely chopped fresh flat-leaf parsley
- ¾ cup extra-virgin olive oil

SERVES 6

1 Make the porridge: Heat oven to 400°F. Toss mushrooms, quartered turnips, 1 tbsp. oil, the garlic, salt, and pepper on a baking sheet and roast until vegetables are golden and slightly crisp and garlic is tender, 25–30 minutes. Set mushrooms and turnips aside; peel garlic and mash into a paste.

2 Heat remaining oil in a 6-qt. Dutch oven over medium. Cook onion until golden, 6–8 minutes. Stir in cracked wheat and cook until slightly toasted, 2–3 minutes. Add wine and cook until reduced by half, about 1 minute. Add 1 cup stock and cook, stirring until absorbed, about 2 minutes. Continue adding stock, 1 cup at a time, and cooking until absorbed before adding more, until wheat is very tender and creamy, about 1 hour total. Meanwhile, melt butter in an 8″ skillet over medium and cook until browned, 8–10 minutes. Stir butter, reserved garlic paste, the Pecorino, salt, and pepper into porridge and keep warm.

3 Make the salsa: Combine vinegar, half the thyme, the chile flakes, shallot, and salt in a bowl and let sit for 20 minutes. Stir in turnip greens, remaining thyme, and the parsley; whisk in oil. Spoon porridge into shallow bowls and top with reserved roasted mushrooms and turnips. Garnish with sliced raw turnips and drizzle salsa over the top.

HERB GARNISHES

Herbs are a simple but delicious way to enhance soups. They can be used singly, for straight-up flavor; in mixtures with other herbs, such as the French classic, *fines herbes*; or as part of a sauce, like pesto. Even the blossoms of herbs can be used, contributing both taste and visual appeal.

FINES HERBES The combination of finely chopped fresh chervil, chives, parsley, and tarragon, known as *fines herbes*, is a hallmark of French cuisine. Use it to garnish carrot soup for a touch of delicate flavor and a refined presentation.

CILANTRO LEAVES & TENDER STEMS People tend to either love or hate cilantro. For those in the pro-cilantro camp, it can be a wonderful garnish for just about any type of soup, from chickpea and lemon, roasted red pepper, and Brazilian black bean to pho. Instead of removing the cilantro stems, leave them attached, as they contain nearly as much flavor as the leaves.

PESTO DI RUCOLA (ARUGULA PESTO) Nothing could be simpler than making fresh pesto. The classic version calls for basil, but swapping in arugula yields a refreshing mixture redolent of springtime flavors. Swirl it into a cold pea soup or a classic minestrone.

PESTO DI PREZZEMOLO (PARSLEY PESTO WITH ANCHOVIES) Not for the faint of heart, this pungent pesto gets a briny boost from capers and anchovies. Do as the Ligurians do and use it to finish a hearty seafood stew or kale soup—and don't forget the crusty bread.

CHIFFONADE OF BASIL It may sound fancy, but a chiffonade of basil is actually a simple technique of slicing basil leaves into thin ribbons. Stack the leaves, tightly roll them up lengthwise into a cylinder, and finely slice with a sharp knife. Now you have an elegant and herbaceous garnish for such basil-friendly recipes as a Tuscan tomato and bread soup or a zucchini soup.

FRIED SAGE & PARSLEY Fried herbs, especially sage, are crisp, richly flavored additions to cold-weather soups. Fried sage is excellent on top of nearly any soup made from a winter vegetable, such as butternut squash, pumpkin, or celery root, while fried parsley complements lighter soups, like curried carrot or chicken and escarole.

HERB FLOWERS Often vendors sell herbs with their flowers, especially at farmers' markets. The flowers have the same essential oils as the herb leaves and stems but are a little milder. Look for the white blossoms of arugula; lavender thyme blossoms, fresh or dried (they have a peppery taste); purple thyme and sage blossoms; and blue rosemary flowers. Pink chive buds and blossoms have a nice spicy flavor. Before you buy, make sure the flowers have not been treated with pesticides.

This rich soup of mushrooms and barley, elevated with fresh thyme and a squeeze of lemon juice, is a more elegant (but no less satisfying) version of the New York deli staple.

CLASSIC MUSHROOM BARLEY SOUP

1	oz. dried porcini mushrooms
1	cup boiling water
¼	cup extra-virgin olive oil
8	cloves garlic, finely chopped
2	medium carrots, finely chopped
2	ribs celery, finely chopped
1	large yellow onion, finely chopped
1	lb. white button mushrooms, thinly sliced
¼	cup sherry
8	cups beef stock
½	cup pearl barley
2	tsp. fresh thyme leaves
2	tbsp. fresh lemon juice
	Kosher salt and freshly ground black pepper, to taste
⅓	cup finely chopped fresh flat-leaf parsley, to garnish

SERVES 8–10

1 Place porcinis in a bowl and cover with boiling water; let sit until softened, about 30 minutes. Using a slotted spoon, transfer mushrooms to a cutting board and finely chop. Pour soaking liquid through a fine-mesh sieve into a bowl, discarding any dirt or sediment. Set mushrooms and soaking liquid aside.

2 Heat oil in a 6-qt. Dutch oven over medium-high. Add garlic, carrots, celery, and onion and cook until soft, about 5 minutes. Add reserved porcini and the white mushrooms and cook, stirring, until mushrooms give off their liquid and it evaporates, about 14 minutes. Add sherry and cook until evaporated, about 2 minutes. Add reserved soaking liquid along with stock, barley, and thyme and bring to a boil. Reduce heat to medium-low and cook, covered and stirring occasionally, until barley is tender, about 30 minutes. Stir in lemon juice and season with salt and pepper. Ladle into bowls and garnish with parsley.

WORKING WITH DRIED MUSHROOMS

Having dried mushrooms in your pantry puts you a couple of steps ahead when it comes to adding a hit of umami to soups and broths.

The first step is to weigh the mushrooms, since recipes usually list the weight rather than a volume measure for dried fungi. Rehydrating comes next; the soaking time varies depending on the type of mushroom you're using. For lighter, less dense varieties like porcini, which are usually packaged thinly sliced, you'll need to leave them submerged in room-temperature water for about a half hour, at which point they should be fully softened. Shiitakes and other denser mushrooms that are sold as whole caps will need quite a bit longer, up to 1 hour.

When the mushrooms are plumped up, squeeze out the liquid and drain them, but don't throw away the soaking water, which has all the heady essence of the fungi. Strain the liquid to remove the grainy residue and use it in the same recipe, or freeze it in cubes for tossing into other dishes. After an optional final cool-water rinse to rid the rehydrated mushrooms of any lingering grit, they are ready to use.

This substantial dish of spiced meat and creamy wheat berries is enjoyed throughout the Persian Gulf and in other parts of the Middle East. There, it is most often made with lamb, but it is particularly delicious when cooked with chicken.

SPICED CHICKEN & WHEAT BERRY PORRIDGE

1½   cups wheat berries, soaked in water overnight and drained

1   cup basmati rice

1   tbsp. kosher salt, plus more to taste

6   tbsp. ghee or clarified butter

1   lb. boneless, skinless chicken thighs, cut into ¼" pieces

Freshly ground black pepper, to taste

6   cloves garlic, finely chopped

1   medium yellow onion, finely chopped

1   2"-piece ginger, peeled and finely chopped

1   cinnamon stick, broken in half

1½   tbsp. bzar (Emirati spice mix)

2   tsp. Aleppo pepper

2   small green Thai chiles, stemmed and finely chopped

1   plum tomato, cored, seeded, and finely chopped

Fried onions, to garnish

SERVES 8–10

1 Bring wheat berries, rice, salt, and 10 cups water to a boil in an 8-qt. saucepan. Reduce heat to medium-low and simmer, stirring occasionally, until wheat berries and rice are very tender and broken down, about 1½ hours.

2 Meanwhile, melt 2 tbsp. ghee in a 6-qt. saucepan over medium-high. Season chicken with salt and pepper and add to pan. Cook, stirring occasionally, until lightly browned, about 5 minutes. Add garlic, onion, ginger, and cinnamon and cook, stirring occasionally, until soft, about 5 minutes. Stir in bzar, 1 tsp. Aleppo pepper, the chiles, and tomato, and cook, stirring occasionally, until fragrant, about 2 minutes. Add 3 cups water and bring to a boil. Reduce heat to medium-low and cook, covered and stirring occasionally, until chicken is tender, about 1 hour.

3 Meanwhile, heat remaining ghee and Aleppo pepper in an 8" skillet over medium-high; cook until fragrant, about 2 minutes. Set spiced ghee aside.

4 Working in batches, transfer the wheat berries, rice, and any cooking liquid to a blender; purée until smooth and return to pan. Stir in chicken mixture over medium; cook, stirring occasionally, for 10 minutes. Ladle stew into bowls and garnish with fried onions. Drizzle spiced ghee over top.

Pozole is a traditional Mexican soup made of hominy, which is dried maize or corn kernels that have been cooked in an alkaline solution and then hulled. Here, the plump kernels swim in a vibrant green broth amped up with a homemade *salsa verde*.

MEXICAN GREEN HOMINY SOUP

1½ lb. tomatillos (about 12), husked, rinsed, and coarsely chopped

2 cups coarsely chopped fresh cilantro leaves and tender stems, plus more to garnish

¼ cup pumpkin seeds, lightly toasted

6 cloves garlic, coarsely chopped

4 scallions, coarsely chopped

2 serrano chiles, stemmed and coarsely chopped

2 cups chicken stock

3 tbsp. canola oil

2 lb. boneless pork shoulder, cut into ½″ pieces

Kosher salt and freshly ground black pepper, to taste

½ cup all-purpose flour

1 large white onion, finely chopped

2 tbsp. ground cumin

2 15-oz. cans hominy, rinsed and drained

¼ small head green cabbage, cored and finely shredded, to garnish

Sliced avocado, to garnish

Chicharrón (fried pork rinds), to garnish (optional)

Lime wedges, for serving

Corn tortillas, warmed, for serving

1 Combine tomatillos, cilantro, pumpkin seeds, garlic, scallions, chiles, and 1 cup stock in a blender. Purée until smooth and set sauce aside.

2 Heat oil in an 8-qt. saucepan over medium-high. Season pork with salt and pepper and toss with flour. Working in batches, cook pork until browned, 6–8 minutes. Return all pork to pan and add onion; cook, stirring occasionally, until onion is golden, 4–6 minutes. Stir in cumin and cook until fragrant, 1–2 minutes. Add remaining stock, the reserved sauce, and the hominy and bring to a boil. Reduce heat to medium-low and cook, covered, until pork is tender, 1½–2 hours.

3 To serve, ladle soup into bowls and garnish with cilantro, cabbage, avocado, and chicharrón. Serve with lime wedges and tortillas.

SERVES 6

Sofrito—the classic aromatic mixture of tomato, onion, and garlic—is the secret to this soup. Here the *sofrito* is puréed and then fried to concentrate the depth of flavor, before the other ingredients are incorporated into the dish.

MEXICAN FAVA BEAN SOUP

2   cups dried fava beans, soaked overnight and drained

1   clove garlic, coarsely chopped

1   ripe tomato, coarsely chopped

½   small yellow onion, coarsely chopped

    Kosher salt and freshly ground black pepper, to taste

1   tbsp. extra-virgin olive oil

¼   tsp. ground cumin

¼   tsp. saffron threads

    Coarsely chopped fresh cilantro leaves, to garnish

SERVES 4

1 Bring fava beans and 4 cups water to a boil in a 4-qt. saucepan. Reduce heat to medium-low; cover and cook, stirring occasionally, until beans are tender, about 40 minutes.

2 Meanwhile, combine garlic, tomato, onion, salt, and pepper in a food processor and purée until smooth; set aside. Heat oil in another 4-qt. saucepan over medium-high. Cook the purée, stirring constantly, until slightly thickened, about 5 minutes. Add the fava beans along with their cooking liquid, the cumin, and saffron. Cook until beans are very tender and break up in the soup, about 10 minutes more. Ladle into bowls and garnish with cilantro.

Native to southwestern France, this robust white bean soup is laced with both bacon and duck confit. As a result, the broth, which is also loaded with root vegetables and sweet Savoy cabbage, has a rustic richness and deep flavor.

CABBAGE & WHITE BEAN SOUP WITH DUCK CONFIT

3   legs duck confit

6   oz. slab bacon, cut into 1/4" matchsticks

8   cloves garlic, finely chopped

2   medium carrots, halved lengthwise and sliced crosswise 1/2" thick

1   medium yellow onion, thinly sliced

1   small leek, trimmed, sliced crosswise 1/2" thick, and rinsed

3/4 cup dry white wine

10 cups chicken stock

1 1/2 cups dried white beans, such as cannellini, Great Northern, or navy, soaked overnight and drained

2   tsp. whole black peppercorns

1   tsp. dried juniper berries

3   sprigs fresh flat-leaf parsley

3   sprigs fresh thyme

2   bay leaves

1   small head Savoy cabbage, cored and thinly sliced

1   large russet potato, peeled and cut into 1/2" pieces

1   large turnip, peeled and cut into 1/2" pieces

Kosher salt and freshly ground black pepper, to taste

Country bread, for serving (optional)

SERVES 8

1 Heat duck legs in an 8-qt. saucepan over medium-high. Cook, flipping once, until fat is rendered and meat is tender, 10–12 minutes. Transfer legs to a cutting board and let cool, then shred meat, discarding skin and bones. Set aside.

2 Add bacon to pan and cook until fat is rendered and bacon is crisp, 5–7 minutes. Using a slotted spoon, transfer bacon to a bowl and set aside. Add garlic, carrots, onion, and leek to pan and cook until golden, about 7 minutes. Add wine and bring to a boil. Cook until reduced by half, 2–3 minutes. Add stock and beans and return to a boil. Place peppercorns, juniper berries, parsley, thyme, and bay leaves on a piece of cheesecloth; tie into a tight bundle and add to pan. Reduce heat to medium-low and cook, partially covered, until beans are very tender, 1–1 1/2 hours.

3 Uncover pan and stir in cabbage, potato, turnip, salt, and pepper and cook until vegetables are tender, about 20 minutes. Stir in reserved duck and bacon and cook for 5 minutes more. Discard herb bundle, ladle soup into bowls, and serve with bread.

In this subtly flavored, creamy lentil stew, the fragrant heat comes from both *nit'r qibe* (a clarified butter made with a variety of spices, such as fenugreek, cumin, and coriander) and *berbere* (the essential Ethiopian dry seasoning featuring numerous spices). The small orange lentils—variously called red lentils, pink lentils, Egyptian lentils, and, in South Asia, *masoor dal*—turn yellow when cooked.

ETHIOPIAN LENTIL STEW

4 tbsp. nit'r qibe (Ethiopian spiced butter) or unsalted butter

1 small yellow onion, finely chopped

4 cloves garlic, finely chopped

1 cup red lentils, rinsed and drained

2 tbsp. berbere (Ethiopian spice mix)

1 small tomato, cored and coarsely chopped

Kosher salt, to taste

SERVES 4-6

Melt spiced butter in a 4-qt. saucepan over medium. Add onion and cook, stirring occasionally, until golden, about 10 minutes. Add garlic and cook until fragrant, 1–2 minutes. Add lentils, 1 tbsp. berbere, the tomato, and 4 cups water. Reduce heat to medium-low and simmer, stirring occasionally, until the lentils are tender and the stew is thickened, 45–50 minutes. Stir in the remaining berbere and season with salt.

In the east Indian state of Odisha, lentil stew is an everyday staple. Based on one prepared at the famed Jagannath Temple in the much-visited town of Puri, this version is fragrant with fresh coconut and sweetened with long-simmered sweet potato. Derived from a giant fennel-like plant, asafoetida imparts garlicky notes to the stew.

LENTIL STEW WITH COCONUT

1 cup toor dal (yellow pigeon peas), rinsed, soaked for 30 minutes, and drained

1 tsp. ground turmeric

1 carrot, cut into 1″ pieces

1 plum tomato, finely chopped

1 small Japanese eggplant, peeled and cut into 1″ pieces

1 small sweet potato, peeled and cut into 1″ pieces

1 small Yukon gold potato, peeled and cut into 1″ pieces

1 2½″ piece ginger, peeled and mashed into a paste

½ small daikon radish, peeled and cut into 1″ pieces

Kosher salt, to taste

1 cup fresh or frozen grated coconut

3 tbsp. sugar

1 tsp. asafoetida

1 morinza oleifera (Indian drumstick), found at Indian markets or online, trimmed and cut into 2″ pieces

¼ cup ghee

1½ tsp. cumin seeds

1 small green Thai chile or ½ serrano, stemmed and halved

SERVES 4–6

1 Bring dal and 8 cups water to a boil in a 6-qt. saucepan. Reduce heat to medium and stir in turmeric, carrot, tomato, eggplant, potatoes, ginger, daikon, and salt; cook until dal is mushy, about 45 minutes. Stir in coconut, sugar, asafoetida, and drumstick and cook until drumstick is tender, 20–25 minutes.

2 Melt ghee in an 8″ skillet over medium-high. Add cumin seeds and chile and cook until seeds pop, 1–2 minutes. Stir melted ghee and seeds into stew, divide between bowls, and serve.

This healthy vegetarian one-pot meal relies on chunks of sweet potatoes, leafy kale, and protein-packed quinoa for heartiness. Almond butter adds nutty richness to the spiced cold-weather soup. To save time, prep the garlic and ginger and measure out the ground spices while the onion is cooking, then add the spices to the onion all at once.

QUINOA & SWEET POTATO SOUP

¼	cup extra-virgin olive oil
1	large red onion, thinly sliced
1	tsp. ground cumin
½	tsp. crushed red chile flakes
½	tsp. ground cinnamon
½	tsp. ground coriander
3	cloves garlic, thinly sliced
1	1" piece ginger, peeled and finely chopped
2	lb. sweet potatoes, peeled and cut into 1" pieces
5	cups vegetable stock
2	cups coarsely chopped kale
½	cup quinoa, rinsed and drained
¼	cup almond butter
	Kosher salt and freshly ground black pepper, to taste

SERVES 6

Heat oil in an 8-qt. saucepan over medium. Cook onion until slightly caramelized, 8 minutes. Stir in cumin, chile flakes, cinnamon, coriander, garlic, and ginger and cook until fragrant, 1–2 minutes. Add sweet potatoes and stock and bring to a boil. Reduce heat to medium and cook until potatoes are tender, 10 minutes. Add kale and quinoa and cook until quinoa is tender, about 20 minutes. Using a ladle, transfer about 1 cup stock from pan into a bowl, whisk in almond butter, and return to pan. Season with salt and pepper and serve.

This richly seasoned, meaty mix called *ghormeh sabzi* (typically translated as "herb stew") is an iconic dish of Iran. Although the types of meat, beans, herbs, and vegetables that go into the pot vary from home to home, the key ingredient, the distinctly floral fenugreek, is a constant. Popular inPersian cooking, dried black limes add sour, citrusy, and earthy flavors. Look for them at Middle Eastern groceries.

IRANIAN VEAL & KIDNEY BEAN STEW

¼ cup canola oil

1 lb. veal shoulder, trimmed and cut into 1″ pieces

Kosher salt and freshly ground black pepper, to taste

1 tbsp. ground turmeric

1 large yellow onion, finely chopped

2 cups finely chopped fresh flat-leaf parsley, plus more to garnish

1½ cups finely chopped fresh cilantro, plus more to garnish

2 bunches scallions, finely chopped

2 cups dried kidney beans, soaked overnight and drained

1½ tbsp. dried fenugreek

4 dried black limes, pierced with a paring knife

Lavash or pita bread, for serving (optional)

SERVES 4-6

Heat oil in a 6-qt. saucepan over medium-high. Season veal with salt and pepper and cook, turning as needed, until browned, about 8 minutes. Using a slotted spoon, transfer veal to a bowl; set aside. Add turmeric and onion to pan and cook, stirring occasionally, until onion is softened, about 10 minutes. Add parsley, cilantro, and scallions and cook until wilted and dark green, about 8 minutes. Add reserved veal, the beans, fenugreek, limes, and 4 cups water and bring to a boil. Reduce heat to medium-low and cook for 10 minutes. Cover partially and continue to cook until veal and beans are tender, about 1½ hours. Discard limes and ladle stew into bowls. Scatter parsley and cilantro over top. Serve with lavash.

This adaptation of a traditional Georgian kidney bean stew includes a creamy purée of toasted walnuts that adds richness and depth to an already hearty Eurasian cold-weather meal. Derived from cayenne, the Holland chile, along with the hot paprika, provides a nice amount of heat.

STEWED RED BEANS & WALNUTS

1	cup walnuts, lightly toasted
½	cup extra-virgin olive oil
6	cloves garlic, finely chopped
1	carrot, finely chopped
1	large yellow onion, finely chopped
1	small red Holland chile, stemmed, seeded, and finely chopped
½	small leek, finely chopped and rinsed
2	tsp. coriander seeds
1	tsp. hot paprika
1	lb. dried dark red kidney beans, soaked overnight and drained
12	cups chicken stock
½	cup finely chopped fresh cilantro
¼	cup finely chopped fresh dill
¼	cup finely chopped fresh flat-leaf parsley
2	tbsp. red wine vinegar
	Kosher salt and freshly ground black pepper, to taste
	Country bread, for serving

SERVES 6–8

Place walnuts and half the oil in a food processor and purée until very smooth; set aside. Heat remaining oil in a 6-qt. saucepan over medium-high. Cook garlic, carrot, onion, chile, and leek, stirring occasionally, until golden, about 10 minutes. Add coriander and paprika and cook until fragrant, about 1 minute. Add beans and stock and bring to a boil. Reduce heat to medium and cook, partially covered, until beans are very tender, 1–1½ hours. Using a ladle, transfer half the beans to a blender; purée until smooth and return to pot. Stir in walnut purée, cilantro, dill, parsley, vinegar, salt, and pepper. Serve with bread on the side.

The popular combination of fatty pork and black beans in this tomato-based Mexican stew is given a potent flavor lift with the addition of hot, fruity habanero chiles. The garnish of shaved baby radishes is both beautiful and functional: It adds brilliant color and a cooling crunch.

PORK & BLACK BEAN STEW

½ cup canola oil

2 lb. boneless pork shoulder, trimmed and cut into 2″ pieces

Kosher salt and freshly ground black pepper, to taste

8 cloves garlic, finely chopped

2 medium white onions, thinly sliced

1 lb. dried black beans, soaked overnight and drained

4 sprigs fresh epazote or cilantro

1 lb. plum tomatoes, cored

2 habanero chiles, stemmed

2 baby radishes, very thinly sliced, to garnish

Fresh cilantro leaves, to garnish

Cooked white rice, for serving

Lime wedges, for serving

SERVES 6-8

1 Heat 2 tbsp. oil in a 6-qt. saucepan over medium-high. Season pork with salt and pepper. Working in batches, cook pork, turning as needed, until browned, about 6 minutes. Using a slotted spoon, transfer pork to a bowl and set aside. Add two-thirds of the garlic and one-quarter of the onions to the pan; cook, stirring occasionally, until soft, about 5 minutes. Return pork to pan. Add beans, epazote, and 8 cups water and bring to a boil. Reduce heat to medium and cook, stirring occasionally, until pork and beans are tender, about 1¼ hours.

2 Meanwhile, heat a 12″ skillet over medium-high. Cook tomatoes and chiles, turning as needed, until blackened all over, about 12 minutes; transfer to a blender. Add the remaining onions and garlic and purée into a smooth sauce. Return skillet to medium-high and add remaining oil. When the oil is hot, fry sauce, stirring constantly, until sauce is slightly reduced, about 8 minutes. Season with salt and pepper and keep sauce warm.

3 To serve, transfer pork and bean stew to a large, deep serving platter and drizzle with reserved sauce. Garnish with radishes and cilantro leaves and serve with rice and lime wedges.

NOODLES
& DUMPLINGS

Chef Danny Bowien, who made his name with his bold take on Chinese food, served this pho as part of a breakfast menu at Mission Cantina in New York City. Bowien believes the flavor goes flat if the broth is cooked too long, so he simmers it for only a short time after bringing it to a boil.

DANNY BOWIEN'S HANOI-STYLE BREAKFAST PHO

1 3½–4-lb. chicken

Kosher salt and freshly ground black pepper, to taste

½ oz. Thai rock sugar or 1 tbsp. granulated sugar

3 tbsp. plus 1 cup fish sauce

2½ lb. fresh wide rice noodles or 32 oz. dried noodles, cooked and drained

1 cup fresh cilantro, stems and leaves, coarsely chopped

4 scallions, thinly sliced

½ large white onion, thinly shaved using a mandoline, rinsed under cold water, and drained

Sriracha sauce, for serving

½ cup fresh lime juice

1 jalapeño chile, stemmed and thinly sliced

SERVES 8

1 Pat chicken dry using paper towels and set on a baking sheet fitted with a rack. Season generously with salt inside and out. Chill, uncovered, overnight.

2 Transfer chicken to a large pot and add 1 gallon water; bring to a boil. Reduce heat to medium and simmer until chicken is cooked through, about 40 minutes. Using tongs, transfer chicken to a cutting board and let cool, then shred meat, discarding skin. Return bones to stock and simmer, skimming as needed, until slightly reduced, 35–40 minutes. Stir in sugar, 3 tbsp. fish sauce, and salt, then strain broth into a clean pot. Add reserved shredded chicken and keep warm.

3 Divide noodles between bowls and top with broth and chicken. Garnish each bowl with some cilantro, scallions, onion, and Sriracha. Combine remaining fish sauce, the lime juice, chile, and pepper in a bowl and serve alongside soup for dipping chicken.

BREAKFAST SOUPS

In many countries, breaking the fast involves a soup—gentle on a sleepy digestive system yet nourishing enough to keep you going until lunchtime or beyond.

MIDDLE EAST & AFRICA Pulses are the base of fragrantly spiced soups like Turkey's *ezo gelin çorbasi*, a vibrant stew of red lentils, bulgur wheat, and tomatoes flavored with dried mint. Tunisians breakfast on *lablabi*, a chickpea-based soup-stew with eye-opening seasonings like cumin and harissa. A morning bowl of peanut, or groundnut, soup is typical in the rural areas of West Africa.

ASIA The Far East and Southeast Asia excel in soup as a morning meal, serving some of the most delicious wake-up calls in the world. China is known for *congee*, a simple rice porridge topped with everything from eggs, meat, vegetables, and fish to peanuts and various condiments. Miso soup with tofu, seaweed, and scallion is an integral component of a full Japanese breakfast. In Myanmar, the day begins with a bowl of *mohinga*, a rice noodle and fish soup, and in tropical Vietnam, pho, rice noodles and beef or chicken in a star anise–scented broth, is the typical morning bowl.

LATIN AMERICA In Mexico, preparing the spicy tripe and hominy soup called menudo is considered an act of love, a labor-intensive gesture for a hungry family. *Changua* is a time-honored start for Colombians, who still happily begin the morning with the milky broth laden with poached eggs, onions, salt, and cilantro.

Wonton soup is ubiquitous in Hong Kong, and the best versions show off generous pink hunks of shrimp through the dumplings' skins. If you prefer, you can fill the wontons with ground chicken or pork.

SHRIMP WONTON SOUP WITH EDAMAME

1 clove garlic, coarsely chopped

1 1″ piece ginger, peeled and coarsely chopped

½ lb. shrimp, peeled and deveined, tails removed, and coarsely chopped

2 tbsp. soy sauce

½ tbsp. Chinese rice wine

1½ tsp. cornstarch

3 scallions (2 finely chopped, 1 thinly sliced)

32 3½″-square wonton wrappers

1 egg, beaten

8 cups chicken stock

1 cup frozen shelled edamame

Hot sesame oil, to garnish

SERVES 8

1 Place garlic and ginger in a food processor and pulse until finely ground. Add shrimp, soy sauce, rice wine, cornstarch, and the finely chopped scallions and pulse until combined. Working with 1 wonton wrapper at a time, place ½ tbsp. filling in center, brush edges lightly with egg, and fold in half, forming a triangle; overlap opposite corners, brushing with egg, and press edges together to seal. Repeat with remaining wrappers and shrimp mixture and chill for up to 1 hour.

2 Bring stock to a boil in an 8-qt. saucepan. Reduce heat to medium-high, add wontons, and cook until firm and cooked through, 4–5 minutes. Stir in edamame. Ladle soup into bowls, garnish with sliced scallions and drizzle with sesame oil.

This popular Peruvian morning dish is garnished in all sorts of ways, with residents of Lima, Peru's capital, often opting for halved hard-cooked eggs. The eggs join hefty whole potatoes, egg noodles, and large chunks of chicken to deliver a hearty, rustic meal.

PERUVIAN CHICKEN NOODLE SOUP

2   carrots, coarsely chopped

2   leeks, white and light green parts only, coarsely chopped and rinsed

2   ribs celery, coarsely chopped

1   5–6-lb. stewing chicken or hen

1   1″ piece ginger, peeled and smashed

1   head garlic, halved crosswise

6   medium Yukon gold potatoes, peeled and left whole

6   oz. dried egg noodles

Kosher salt and freshly ground black pepper, to taste

FOR SERVING

2   tbsp. coarsely chopped fresh cilantro

6   hard-cooked eggs, peeled and halved

4   scallions, thinly sliced

2   limes, quartered

1   fresh red chile, such as Fresno, stemmed, seeded, and finely chopped

SERVES 6

1 Combine carrots, leeks, celery, chicken, ginger, garlic, and 5 qt. cold water in an 8-qt. saucepan and bring to a boil. Reduce heat to medium-low and cook, skimming occasionally, until chicken is cooked through or an instant-read thermometer inserted into thigh reads 165°F, and the stock has become rich and golden, about 3½ hours. Using tongs, transfer chicken to a cutting board and let cool. Strain stock through a fine-mesh sieve set over a bowl and discard vegetables; return stock to pan.

2 Add potatoes to stock, bring to a simmer over medium-high, and cook until potatoes are tender, about 25 minutes. Meanwhile, shred chicken into at least 6 large pieces, discarding skin and bones.

3 Bring the broth to a boil. Cook egg noodles until al dente, about 10 minutes. Add the reserved chicken pieces and season with salt and pepper; cook until chicken is warmed through.

4 To serve, ladle soup into bowls and garnish with cilantro, eggs, scallions, limes, and chile.

A specialty of the southwestern German region of Swabia, this dish marries a pure, simple broth with ravioli-like dumplings filled with a spinach-laced mix of minced beef, pork, veal, and bacon.

GERMAN-STYLE DUMPLINGS IN BROTH

FOR THE DUMPLING DOUGH

- 1½ cups all-purpose flour
- 2 tbsp. durum wheat (semolina) flour
- ½ tsp. canola oil
- 3 eggs, lightly beaten

FOR THE DUMPLING GARNISH

- 1 tbsp. canola oil
- 1 small yellow onion, finely chopped
- 2 tbsp. finely chopped fresh flat-leaf parsley

FOR THE DUMPLING FILLING

- 3 oz. ground beef
- 3 oz. ground pork
- 3 oz. ground veal
- 1½ oz. bacon, finely chopped
- ¼ cup finely chopped fresh flat-leaf parsley
- 2 tbsp. finely chopped cooked spinach
- 2 tbsp. heavy cream
- 2 eggs, lightly beaten
- ¼ small yellow onion, finely chopped

  Freshly grated nutmeg, to taste

  Kosher salt and freshly ground black pepper, to taste

FOR THE SOUP

- 6 cups chicken stock
- ¼ cup finely chopped carrot
- ¼ cup finely chopped celery

  Kosher salt and freshly ground black pepper, to taste

SERVES 8

1 Make the dumpling dough: Whisk both flours in a bowl. Add oil and eggs and stir until dough forms. Transfer dough to a lightly floured work surface and knead until smooth, 4–6 minutes. Divide dough into 4 balls and wrap individually in plastic wrap. Chill for 1 hour.

2 Make the dumpling garnish: Heat oil in an 8″ skillet over medium and cook onion, stirring occasionally, until caramelized, about 25 minutes; set aside.

3 Make the dumpling filling: Mix beef, pork, veal, bacon, parsley, spinach, cream, half the beaten eggs, the onion, nutmeg, salt, and pepper in a bowl. Transfer mixture to a piping bag fitted with a ½″ round tip and set aside.

4 Using a pasta roller, and working with 1 dough ball at a time, roll dough until ¹⁄₁₆″ thick. Lay 1 sheet of pasta lengthwise on a work surface and pipe one-quarter of the filling in a straight line down the lower third of the pasta sheet. Roll pasta up and over filling and brush edges with remaining egg to seal; trim excess dough. Use a knife sharpening steel or the handle of a wooden spoon to press down on dough at 2″ intervals to create dumplings, rolling steel back and forth to seal dough in between dumplings; use a paring knife to separate dumplings. Continue with remaining pasta and filling to make about 25 dumplings.

5 Bring a 6-qt. pot of water to a boil. Working in batches, cook dumplings until they float, about 20 minutes; set aside.

6 Make the soup: Bring chicken stock, carrot, celery, salt, and pepper to a simmer in a 6-qt. saucepan over medium-high and cook until vegetables are soft, about 3 minutes. Divide dumplings between bowls and ladle soup over top. Garnish dumplings with some of the caramelized onions and parsley.

ASIAN NOODLES

Scouring Asian grocery stores for noodles can be daunting—the choices seem endless and the labeling wildly varied. The easiest way to differentiate Asian noodles is by their main ingredients, as a number of the types are sold in various widths and are used in more than one Asian cuisine. Most Asian soup noodles can be divided into three ingredient categories: wheat and buckwheat, rice, and vegetable starch.

WHEAT NOODLES are the largest category of Asian noodles and are typically made from wheat flour and water, and sometimes egg, salt, and other additives. They can vary widely in taste, texture, and chewiness and are sold fresh (soft) or dried. They also come flat, wide, round, thick, or thin. Generally used in hot soups, wheat noodles include everything from long, thin wonton noodles, made from the same dough used to make wonton wrappers; hand-pulled fresh Chinese lo mein noodles; udon, the thickest and chewiest of the bunch and prized for their ample bite; and ramen, thin, curly, and served with meat and vegetables. The best ramen is sold fresh and is worth seeking out, but the most common ones are found dried and compressed into a brick.

BUCKWHEAT NOODLES are a subcategory of wheat noodles, since they contain both buckwheat and wheat flour. Soba, the most widely recognizable buckwheat noodle, is a thin Japanese noodle with a distinctive taste. Soba is popular in both cold and hot soups. *Naengmyeon* are Korean noodles that are often made with buckwheat and added starch like sweet potato or arrowroot and are typically used in cold, broth-based noodle soups. (Despite the name, buckwheat is the seed of a flowering fruit and is not related to wheat, nor is it even a grain. Buckwheat noodles almost always contain wheat flour because otherwise they would break too easily.)

RICE VERMICELLI and wider rice "sticks" are made from rice, rice flour, or rice powder. These popular noodles are used as the base of many Thai soups, like spicy *laksa*, and most notably in Vietnamese pho. They are ideal for soaking up bold flavors and cook quickly and easily.

CELLOPHANE, OR GLASS, NOODLES are most commonly made from mung bean and sometimes from yam or potato starch, and are the size of vermicelli. These quick-cooking noodles (they need only a minute or less in hot water to cook) are often served with a brightly flavored broth topped with chile oil and ground meat.

Pandanus leaves, either fresh or frozen, lend an earthy sweetness to the stock in this richly spiced noodle soup. The addition of fresh pig's or beef blood, available from most butchers, adds a unique silken texture and depth of flavor. The recipe is inspired by a soup Andy Ricker served at Pok Pok, his Thai restaurant in Portland.

THAI BOAT NOODLE SOUP

FOR THE BROTH

2½	lb. boneless pork shoulder, trimmed and cut into 1" pieces
2	oz. Thai rock sugar or ¼ cup granulated sugar
10	cups pork stock or water
¾	cup light soy sauce
1	tbsp. dark soy sauce
1	tbsp. whole black peppercorns
10	sprigs fresh cilantro
4	bay leaves
3	stalks lemongrass, trimmed and thinly sliced
2	fresh or frozen pandanus leaves
2	stalks Chinese or regular celery, cut into 3" pieces
2	star anise
1	1½" piece fresh or frozen galangal, peeled and thinly sliced
1	stick cinnamon

FOR THE SOUP

10	oz. frozen Thai pork balls
10	oz. thin, flat rice noodles, soaked in warm water for 15 minutes and drained
½	lb. boneless pork shoulder, sliced into 1" strips about ⅛" thick
2	stalks Chinese or regular celery, leaves and tender stalks coarsely chopped
2	oz. Chinese or regular spinach, stemmed and chopped
1½	cups bean sprouts

FOR SERVING

3	tbsp. canola oil
3	cloves garlic, finely chopped
4	tsp. granulated sugar
4	tsp. pig's or beef blood
¼	cup packed fresh cilantro leaves
¼	cup nam pla (Thai fish sauce)
¼	cup vinegar-pickled Thai chiles, stemmed and thinly sliced, plus ¼ cup pickling juice
4	tsp. ancho chile powder

SERVES 8

1 Make the broth: Combine all ingredients in an 8-qt. saucepan and bring to a boil. Reduce heat to medium-low and cook, covered, until pork is tender, about 1 hour. Strain broth into a bowl. Using tongs, transfer pork to broth and discard solids; keep warm.

2 Make the soup: Bring a large pot of water to a boil. Add pork balls, rice noodles, sliced pork shoulder, and celery and cook until pork is cooked through, 4–6 minutes. Add spinach and bean sprouts and cook for 30 seconds more.

3 Meanwhile, heat oil and garlic in a 1-qt. saucepan over medium-low and cook until garlic is golden, 6–8 minutes. To serve, divide soup between bowls. Top with reserved broth and pork and garlic oil. Stir sugar and blood into each bowl and top with cilantro, nam pla, chiles, and chile powder.

Slow-simmered chicken stock gets a boost of flavor with the addition of pan-seared ground pork seasoned with ginger, garlic, spicy Japanese chile bean sauce, and nutty sesame paste. It's a rich base for a steaming bowl of ramen noodles. A tangle of shredded scallions adds a crisp finish.

TANTANMEN RAMEN

1   lb. chicken wings

12   cups chicken stock

1   tbsp. toasted sesame oil

2   tbsp. finely chopped scallions, plus ¼ cup, thinly sliced, to garnish

1   clove garlic, finely chopped

1   1½" piece ginger, peeled and finely chopped

½   lb. ground pork

1   tbsp. tobanjan (Japanese chile bean sauce)

2   tbsp. soy sauce

1   tsp. sugar

¼   cup plus 1 tbsp. nerigoma (Japanese sesame paste)

2   tsp. kosher salt, plus more for salting

1   lb. fresh or defrosted frozen ramen noodles

   Rayu (Japanese hot chile oil), for serving

SERVES 4

1 Place chicken wings and stock in an 8-qt. saucepan over medium. Bring to a simmer and cook, skimming foam, until stock is reduced to about 8 cups, 3–3½ hours. Strain, discarding solids; reserve stock.

2 Heat oil, finely chopped scallions, garlic, and ginger in a 12" skillet over medium-high. Cook, stirring occasionally, until fragrant, about 2 minutes. Add pork and tobanjan and cook, breaking up meat into small pieces, until pork is cooked through, 5–6 minutes. Add reserved stock, soy sauce, sugar, nerigoma, and salt; bring to a boil. Reduce heat to medium and cook, stirring, for 3 minutes more; keep soup warm.

3 Meanwhile, bring a pot of generously salted water to a boil. Add noodles and cook until tender, 2–3 minutes; drain and divide between 4 deep soup bowls. Ladle soup over each bowl of noodles. Garnish with thinly sliced scallions and a drizzle of rayu.

HOW TO EAT RAMEN

Ramen is typically eaten with chopsticks held in the dominant hand and a dipper-shaped spoon in the other hand. The most important thing is to start eating as soon as the soup arrives and to eat quickly, or the broth will become tepid and the noodles mushy. To eat the noodles, grab a small bunch from the bowl with your chopsticks, making sure they are cleanly separated from the rest, and briefly dip them back in the broth. Then, slurp them quickly and loudly into your mouth (the noise is considered polite). Chase bites of noodles with spoonfuls of broth and pieces of the toppings, like roast pork, scallions, or hard-cooked egg. When the noodles and toppings are gone, bring the bowl to your mouth and drink down the broth.

Making authentic Tokyo-style ramen at home is not for the impatient cook, but the satisfying results are well worth the time and effort. This luscious, aromatic dish has a soy sauce–enriched broth, tender pork, fragrant scallions, earthy bamboo shoots, creamy egg, and more.

SHOYU RAMEN

2	lb. bone-in chicken thighs
2	lb. pork knuckles and rib bones
2	tsp. kosher salt
16	cloves garlic
1	leek, green part only, chopped and rinsed
1	small yellow onion, quartered
1	4″ piece kombu
1	2″ piece ginger, peeled and sliced
6	oz. dried bamboo shoots, cut into 3″ pieces
1½	lb. pork flank steak
⅔	cup soy sauce
2	tbsp. sake
½	cup mirin
2	oz. pork fat
3	tbsp. canola oil
13	oz. dried chuka soba noodles
4–6	soft-boiled eggs, halved lengthwise
1	nori sheet, cut into 8 rectangles
2	scallions, thinly sliced on an angle

SERVES 4-6

1 Combine chicken, pork knuckles and bones, 1 tsp. salt, 8 cloves garlic, the leek, onion, kombu, half the ginger, and 12 cups water in an 8-qt. saucepan over medium-high. Bring to a boil, then reduce heat to medium and simmer, partially covered, for 4 hours. Strain, discarding solids; keep ramen broth warm.

2 Meanwhile, soak bamboo shoots in water for 3 hours; drain, discard soaking water, and set aside.

3 Combine the remaining salt and ginger, 3 cloves garlic, the flank steak, soy sauce, sake, and 1 cup water in a 2-qt. saucepan over high. Bring to a boil, then reduce heat to medium and simmer, covered, for 40 minutes. Let pork cool, then strain; transfer pork to a cutting board and reserve this chasu broth. Thinly slice pork and set aside. Keep chasu broth warm.

4 Combine reserved bamboo shoots, ½ cup reserved chasu broth, the mirin, and 1 cup water in a small saucepan over high. Bring to a boil, then reduce heat to medium and simmer, covered, for 30 minutes. Drain, discard cooking liquid, and set aside.

5 Combine remaining garlic and the pork fat in a food processor and process to form a smooth paste. Heat oil in a small skillet over medium-high. Reduce heat to medium-low and add the garlic paste; cook, stirring, until garlic is barely golden, about 8 minutes. Remove from heat and set aside.

6 Heat ramen broth in an 8-qt. saucepan over medium-high; add noodles and cook, stirring, until soft, about 4 minutes.

7 To serve, divide ramen broth and noodles between bowls. Top with bamboo shoots, sliced pork flank, reserved chasu broth, garlic paste, eggs, nori, and scallions.

When the Acadians were forced out of French Canada in the late 1700s, many of them flocked to Louisiana, bringing a rich culinary heritage along with them; it would eventually become the Cajun food we know today. In this classic Acadian comfort dish called *fricot,* fresh savory—a pungent, peppery herb—adds a piney zest to the dumplings, which puff up when they are dropped into the simmering soup.

ACADIAN CHICKEN & DUMPLINGS

FOR THE SOUP

- 4 tbsp. unsalted butter
- 1 tsp. extra-virgin olive oil
- 2 lb. boneless, skinless chicken thighs

  Kosher salt and freshly ground black pepper, to taste
- 3 cloves garlic, coarsely chopped
- 1 large yellow onion, finely chopped
- 1 medium carrot, coarsely chopped
- 1 rib celery, coarsely chopped
- 6 cups chicken stock
- 4 sprigs savory
- 1 large russet potato, peeled and cut into 1″ pieces

FOR THE DUMPLINGS

- 1 cup flour
- 1 tbsp. finely chopped fresh savory
- 2 tsp. baking powder
- ½ tsp. kosher salt
- ½ cup milk

SERVES 8

1 Make the soup: Heat butter and oil in a 6-qt. saucepan over medium-high. Season chicken with salt and pepper; working in batches, cook, flipping once, until browned, 5–7 minutes. Using tongs, transfer chicken to a plate and set aside. Add garlic, onion, carrot, and celery to pan and cook, stirring occasionally, until soft, about 7 minutes. Return chicken and any juices to pan with stock and savory and bring to a boil. Reduce heat to medium-low and cook, covered, until chicken is tender, 8–10 minutes. Add potato and cook until tender, about 8 minutes more. Using tongs, transfer chicken to a cutting board and let cool; discard savory. When chicken is cool, shred into large pieces and return to pan. Return soup to a simmer over medium.

2 Make the dumplings: Whisk flour, savory, baking powder, and salt in a bowl. Stir in milk until a thick batter forms. Drop a 1-oz. scoop or 2 tablespoonfuls each of batter into simmering soup. When dumplings are puffed and slightly firm, cover pan and continue to cook for 5 minutes more. Divide soup and dumplings between bowls and serve.

The rustic noodle soup *ash-e reshteh* is typically served in late March to celebrate Nowruz, the Persian New Year, because noodles symbolize good fortune. You can purchase Iranian *reshteh*—flat, narrow wheat noodles—in Middle Eastern shops or online. Linguine can be substituted.

IRANIAN NOODLE SOUP

½ cup canola oil

2 small yellow onions, thinly sliced

½ cup dried kidney beans, soaked overnight and drained

½ cup dried cannellini beans, soaked overnight and drained

½ cup dried chickpeas, soaked overnight and drained

1½ tbsp. ground turmeric

Kosher salt and freshly ground black pepper, to taste

6 cups finely chopped spinach

1 cup finely chopped fresh flat-leaf parsley

½ cup brown lentils

1 bunch chives, finely chopped

2 cups reshteh or linguini

8 cloves garlic, thinly sliced

2 tbsp. dried mint

¼ cup whey powder

SERVES 6–8

1 Heat ¼ cup oil in an 8-qt. saucepan over medium-high. Cook onions until caramelized, about 20 minutes. Transfer half the onions to a bowl and set aside for garnish. Add all the soaked legumes, the turmeric, salt, and pepper to onions in pan and cook, stirring, for 5 minutes. Add 12 cups water and bring to a boil. Reduce heat to medium-low and cook, covered, until legumes are barely tender, about 50 minutes. Stir in spinach, parsley, lentils, and chives and cook for 20 minutes. Add noodles and cook until noodles and beans are tender, about 12 minutes.

2 Meanwhile, heat remaining oil in a 10″ skillet over medium-high. Cook garlic until golden and crisp, about 3 minutes. Using a slotted spoon, transfer garlic chips to paper towels to drain. Return skillet to medium-high and add mint. Cook until fragrant, about 1 minute, then set aside to cool. Combine whey powder and 4 tbsp. water in a small bowl. Swirl mint oil into whey mixture.

3 Ladle soup into bowls and garnish with reserved caramelized onions and garlic chips. Drizzle with the whey–mint oil.

Fideos, the Spanish word for "noodles," usually refers specifically to the thin, vermicelli-like wheat noodles popular in Mexico and Spain. In this recipe, the noodles are cooked right in the soup, helping to thicken the broth, while crumbly *queso fresco* provides a creaminess that counters the acidity of the tomatoes.

MEXICAN NOODLE SOUP

¼ cup canola oil

4 cloves garlic, finely chopped

3 medium carrots, finely chopped

3 ribs celery, finely chopped

1 medium white onion, finely chopped

6 cups chicken stock

1 28-oz. can whole peeled tomatoes, crushed by hand

2 oz. fideos or vermicelli, broken into 2″ pieces

½ lb. queso fresco or feta, crumbled

¼ cup thinly sliced fresh flat-leaf parsley, to garnish (optional)

SERVES 6–8

Heat oil in a 4-qt. saucepan over medium. Cook garlic, carrots, celery, and onion, stirring occasionally, until soft, about 10 minutes. Add stock and tomatoes and bring to a boil. Reduce heat to medium-low and cook, stirring occasionally, until tomatoes break down completely, about 1 hour. Pour soup through a fine-mesh sieve into a bowl; discard solids and return soup to pan over medium-high. Add fideos and cook, stirring occasionally, until al dente, about 4 minutes. Divide queso fresco between bowls and ladle soup over top. Garnish with parsley.

These dumplings have a surprising meatiness. The secret ingredient: bone marrow. Clear beef broth, along with julienned carrots and leeks, offers a clean foil to the richness of the marrow dumplings in this simple yet satisfying soup.

BEEF MARROW DUMPLING SOUP

FOR THE DUMPLINGS

- 6 oz. kaiser rolls (about 2)
  Warm water, as needed
- 2½ cups bread crumbs
- 6 tbsp. finely chopped fresh flat-leaf parsley, plus more to garnish
- 2 eggs, lightly beaten
- ¼ tsp. freshly grated nutmeg
  Kosher salt and freshly ground black pepper, to taste
- 1¼ lb. beef marrow bones

FOR THE BROTH

- 10 cups beef stock
- 1 small carrot, julienned
- 1 small leek, white part only, julienned and rinsed
  Kosher salt and freshly ground black pepper, to taste

SERVES 8

1 Make the dumplings: Place rolls in a bowl and cover with warm water. Let sit until soft, about 30 minutes, then drain and squeeze completely dry. Using your fingers, crumble rolls into a medium bowl. Add bread crumbs, parsley, the eggs, nutmeg, salt, and pepper and set aside. Using a small spoon or butter knife, scoop marrow from bones into a small saucepan and melt over medium. Pour into bowl with rolls and mix until dough forms. Using wet hands, divide bread mixture into about 30 balls and set aside.

2 Make the broth: Combine stock, carrot, leek, salt, and pepper in a 6-qt. saucepan and bring to a boil. Reduce heat to medium and add dumplings. Cook, stirring occasionally, until dumplings are cooked through, about 3 minutes. Ladle soup and dumplings into bowls and garnish with parsley.

This recipe comes from the Bohemian Café, a Eurocentric family restaurant that helped put Omaha, Nebraska, on the culinary map. Its take on a classic Czech soup uses chicken livers instead of the more traditional beef, and bread crumbs made from kaiser rolls serve as the base for the dumplings.

BOHEMIAN CHICKEN LIVER DUMPLING SOUP

½ lb. kaiser rolls (about 3), thinly sliced

3 tbsp. extra-virgin olive oil

1 small yellow onion, finely chopped

3 cloves garlic, finely chopped

4 oz. chicken livers, trimmed and finely chopped

Kosher salt and freshly ground black pepper, to taste

½ cup milk

⅓ cup finely chopped fresh flat-leaf parsley

¼ cup flour

½ tsp. freshly grated nutmeg

2 eggs, lightly beaten

8 cups beef stock

SERVES 6

1 Heat oven to 325°F. Spread sliced rolls in single layers on 2 baking sheets and bake until slightly dry, about 12 minutes. Let toasted slices cool, then transfer to a food processor and pulse into fine bread crumbs. Transfer to a large bowl and set aside.

2 Heat oil in a 12″ skillet over medium-high. Cook onion, stirring occasionally, until golden, 4–5 minutes. Add garlic and cook until fragrant, 1–2 minutes. Stir in livers and season with salt and pepper; cook until tender, about 3 minutes. Transfer liver mixture to bowl with bread crumbs. Add milk to skillet and bring to a boil; pour milk over bread and liver mixture. Add ¼ cup parsley, the flour, nutmeg, eggs, salt, and pepper and stir until combined. Cover with plastic wrap and chill for 30 minutes.

3 Bring stock to a boil in a 6-qt. saucepan. Reduce heat to medium and cook until reduced to 6 cups, 10–12 minutes; keep warm. Meanwhile, bring an 8-qt. saucepan of water to a boil. Using wet hands, divide reserved dumpling mixture into 6 balls and add to boiling water; cook until dumplings are firm, 4 minutes. Using a slotted spoon, transfer dumplings to bowls. Ladle broth over top, and garnish with remaining parsley.

This borlotti bean stew with shell-like gnocchi, called *pisarei*, originates in the Italian town of Piacenza, where, legend has it, mothers would look at the hands of a son's intended bride to make sure she had the calluses that come from dragging dough across a wooden board to shape gnocchi. A fresh herb sauce laced with *speck* (Italian cured meat) tops off the stew in this recipe from chef Jenn Louis.

GNOCCHI & BORLOTTI BEAN STEW WITH PARSLEY-SPECK PESTO

FOR THE GNOCCHI

- 1½ cups flour, plus more for dusting
- 1 cup dried bread crumbs
- 2 tsp. kosher salt
- 1 cup boiling water, plus more as needed

FOR THE PESTO

- 1½ cups packed fresh flat-leaf parsley leaves
- ⅔ cup extra-virgin olive oil
- ¼ tsp. crushed red chile flakes
- 2 cloves garlic
- 2 oz. speck or prosciutto, finely chopped
- ¼ cup finely grated Parmigiano-Reggiano
  Kosher salt, to taste

FOR THE STEW

- 2 tbsp. extra-virgin olive oil
- 2 tbsp. fresh rosemary leaves
- 1 4-oz. piece lardo or pancetta, cut into ¼" pieces
- 1 small yellow onion, finely chopped
- 1 carrot, finely chopped
- 1 bay leaf
- ½ cup dry red wine
- 8 cups beef or vegetable stock

- 1¼ cups dried borlotti or cranberry beans, soaked overnight and drained
- 2 tbsp. finely chopped fresh flat-leaf parsley
- ½ cup finely grated Parmigiano-Reggiano, plus more for serving
- 6 tbsp. unsalted butter, cubed
- 1 16-oz. can whole peeled tomatoes, puréed

SERVES 6

1 Make the gnocchi: Pulse flour, bread crumbs, and salt in a food processor until combined. With the motor running, slowly add the boiling water and mix until dough forms. If dough is dry, add more boiling water, 1 tbsp. at a time, until a firm dough forms. Transfer dough to an unfloured surface and knead briefly until dough is smooth. Quarter dough and cover loosely with plastic wrap. Working with a quarter of the dough at a time, use your hands to roll dough into a ½"-thick rope. Cut dough crosswise into ½" pieces. Working with one piece at a time, press down on the dough with the side of your thumb while rolling and flicking up to create gnocchi. Transfer gnocchi to a flour-dusted, parchment paper–lined baking sheet. Separate gnocchi to prevent sticking and cover with plastic wrap. Chill until ready to use.

2 Make the pesto: Purée parsley, oil, chile flakes, and garlic in a food processor until smooth and transfer to a bowl. Stir in speck, Parmigiano, and salt and set aside.

3 Make the stew: Heat oil in an 8-qt. saucepan over medium. Cook rosemary, lardo, onion, carrot, and bay leaf until vegetables are soft, 4–6 minutes. Raise heat to medium-high and add wine; cook until reduced by half, 1–2 minutes. Add stock, beans, parsley, and 2 cups water and bring to a boil. Reduce heat to medium and cook, covered, until beans are tender, 1½–2 hours. Add reserved gnocchi, the Parmigiano, butter, and tomato purée; simmer until gnocchi are cooked through, about 15 minutes. Discard bay leaf. Ladle stew into bowls and garnish with reserved pesto and more Parmigiano.

The key to producing this robust golden broth is taking the time to brown the chicken wings and beef bones properly. The *sucs,* or browned caramelized bits that result from this step, are left in the pan to enhance the flavor of the broth. You could enjoy the broth on its own, but adding the *crespelle* (savory herbed crêpes) makes it that much better.

CRESPELLE EN BRODO

FOR THE BRODO

- 2 tbsp. extra-virgin olive oil
- 3 lb. chicken wings
- 1 lb. beef bones, cut into 2″ pieces (ask your butcher to do this)
- 2 carrots, coarsely chopped
- 2 large yellow onions, coarsely chopped
- 2 ribs celery, coarsely chopped
- 1 clove garlic, unpeeled and crushed
- 3 sprigs fresh flat-leaf parsley
- 1 bay leaf
- 1 plum tomato, cored and halved

FOR THE CRESPELLE & SERVING

- ¼ cup finely chopped fresh flat-leaf parsley, plus more to garnish
- 5 tbsp. all-purpose flour
- 1 tbsp. grated Parmigiano-Reggiano, plus more to garnish
- 1 tbsp. extra-virgin olive oil
- ¼ tsp. freshly grated nutmeg
- 5 eggs
- Freshly ground black pepper, for serving

SERVES 6-8

1 Make the brodo: Heat oil in a 6-qt. Dutch oven over medium-high. Working in batches, cook chicken wings and beef bones until browned, 35–40 minutes; transfer to a bowl. Add carrots, onions, celery, and garlic to pan and cook until golden, 6–8 minutes. Return wings and bones to pan. Add parsley, bay leaf, tomato, and 20 cups water; simmer, skimming as needed, for 4 hours. Strain through a fine-mesh sieve into a clean saucepan and discard solids; keep warm.

2 Make the crespelle: Whisk parsley, flour, Parmigiano, oil, nutmeg, eggs, and 1 cup water in a bowl until smooth. Heat an 8″ nonstick skillet over medium-high. Working in batches, pour 2 tbsp. batter into skillet while tilting skillet to let batter cover bottom completely. Cook until crespelle is golden on the bottom, 1–2 minutes. Flip and cook for 1 minute more; transfer to a plate. Roll each crespelle into a cigar shape. To serve, divide crespelle cigars between shallow bowls and ladle reserved brodo over top. Garnish with parsley, Parmigiano, and pepper.

CHILLED

Spinach and chives are blended with ice cubes to ensure that this chilled yogurt-based soup keeps its bright green color. The light, creamy blend is lavishly garnished with toasted bread crumbs, chopped chives, deeply charred scallions, and a little grated horseradish.

SPRING HERB & YOGURT SOUP WITH GRILLED SCALLIONS

4	tbsp. unsalted butter
4	oz. dark rye bread, pulsed into coarse crumbs in a food processor
2	cups packed baby spinach
¾	cup coarsely chopped chives, plus 2 tbsp. finely chopped, to garnish
½	cup ice cubes
	Kosher salt and freshly ground black pepper, to taste
1½	cups plain, full-fat Greek yogurt
¾	cup heavy cream
18	scallions, trimmed and halved lengthwise
3	tbsp. canola oil
1	2-oz. piece fresh horseradish, peeled

SERVES 4

1 Melt butter in a 12″ skillet over medium. Cook bread crumbs until crisp, 4–5 minutes; transfer to paper towels to drain. Purée the spinach, coarsely chopped chives, ice cubes, salt, pepper, and 2 cups water in a blender until smooth; strain through a fine-mesh sieve into a bowl, discard solids, and stir in yogurt. In a separate bowl, beat cream until stiff peaks form; fold in yogurt mixture. Cover soup with plastic wrap and chill until ready to serve.

2 Build a medium-hot fire in a charcoal grill or heat a gas grill to medium-high. (Alternatively, heat oven broiler.) Toss scallions with oil, salt, and pepper on a baking sheet; grill, turning as needed, until slightly charred, 1–2 minutes. Ladle soup into bowls. Garnish with reserved bread crumbs and finely chopped chives, top with grilled scallions, and grate horseradish over the top.

The flavors of Morocco—warm spices, fresh citrus, and fragrant orange-flower water—enliven this refreshing carrot-ginger blend. Although this colorful soup can be enjoyed at room temperature, it tastes best when served well chilled.

MOROCCAN-SPICED CARROT-GINGER SOUP

2	tbsp. extra-virgin olive oil
2½	lb. carrots, peeled
1	3" piece ginger, peeled and coarsely chopped
½	tsp. ground cinnamon
½	tsp. ground cumin
¼	tsp. ground ginger
	Pinch cayenne
	Pinch freshly grated nutmeg
1	cup fresh orange juice
1	tsp. orange-flower water
	Kosher salt, to taste
	Yogurt, for serving

SERVES 4-6

Heat oil in a medium saucepan over medium. Add carrots and ginger and cook until soft, 15 minutes. Meanwhile, combine cinnamon, cumin, ginger, cayenne, and nutmeg in a 10" skillet over medium and cook until fragrant, about 1 minute. Add orange juice and 1 cup water and simmer until reduced by half, 20 minutes; let cool. Stir spiced orange juice and orange-flower water into carrot-ginger soup and season with salt. Transfer to a blender and purée until smooth. Cover with plastic wrap and chill until ready to serve. Ladle chilled soup into bowls and top with a dollop of yogurt.

Spanish white gazpachos are typically almond-based, but this luscious soup calls for sweet macadamia nuts instead. The nuts are toasted to deepen their flavor and then blended along with several other ingredients into a rich, smooth, velvety base.

MACADAMIA GAZPACHO WITH CURED ASPARAGUS

3½	cups raw unsalted macadamia nuts
1¼	cups extra-virgin olive oil
6	oz. stale sourdough bread, crusts removed, coarsely chopped
5	cups ice-cold water
2	tbsp. kosher salt
1	tsp. plus 1 tbsp. honey
	Grated zest of 1 lime, plus ¾ cup juice
2	cloves garlic
¼	cup coarsely chopped fresh flowering cilantro or regular cilantro leaves and stems, plus whole leaves to garnish
1	small serrano chile, stemmed, seeded, and finely chopped
10	oz. asparagus, trimmed, peeled, and sliced ¾″ thick on the bias

SERVES 6

1 Toast nuts in a 12″ skillet over medium-high; transfer to a blender. Heat ¼ cup oil in skillet over medium; add bread and cook until golden and crisp, 4–5 minutes. Let bread cool, then transfer to blender. Add half the water and salt, 1 tsp. honey, the lime zest and ¼ cup juice, and garlic and purée just until smooth. Add remaining water, and, with the motor running, slowly pour in ½ cup oil. Purée until soup is emulsified, then chill until ready to serve.

2 Whisk the remaining salt, honey, and lime juice, the chopped cilantro, and chile in a bowl. While whisking, slowly drizzle in remaining oil until vinaigrette is emulsified. Stir in asparagus and cover with plastic wrap; chill 30 minutes before serving. To serve, ladle chilled soup into glasses or bowls. Spoon asparagus mixture over top and garnish with cilantro leaves.

Known in Mexico as *sopa de poro y papa,* this creamy Mexico City favorite speaks to the comforting, diverse cuisine of the nation. In summer, serve it chilled, in a nod to French vichyssoise, but it's also good served hot on a cold night.

CHILLED MEXICAN POTATO-LEEK SOUP

4 tbsp. unsalted butter

3 medium leeks, white and light green parts only, coarsely chopped and rinsed

2 medium white onions, coarsely chopped

1 medium russet potato, peeled and coarsely chopped

8 cups vegetable or chicken stock

1 bay leaf

Kosher salt and freshly ground black pepper, to taste

½ cup crema or sour cream, to garnish

2 tbsp. finely chopped chives, to garnish

Extra-virgin olive oil, to garnish

Grilled bread, for serving (optional)

SERVES 8-10

1 Melt butter in a 4-qt. saucepan over medium. Cook leeks, onions, and potato, stirring occasionally, until soft, about 20 minutes. Add stock and bay leaf and simmer, stirring occasionally, until potato is mushy, about 35 minutes. Season with salt and pepper. Working in batches, purée soup in a blender until smooth. Transfer soup to a pitcher or bowl and chill for 2 hours.

2 Ladle chilled soup into bowls. Garnish with a swirl of crema, a sprinkling of chives, and a drizzle of oil. Serve with grilled bread.

Okroshka is thought to come from the Russian word for "small pieces," which is the defining texture of this chilled soup of chopped vegetables and beef. The final addition of *kvass,* a fermented drink made from rye bread, turns this into a refreshing antidote to the heat of summer.

RUSSIAN CHILLED VEGETABLE SOUP

Kosher salt, to taste

3 carrots, peeled and cut into ¼" pieces

1 lb. waxy potatoes, peeled and cut into ¼" pieces

16 scallions, white and light green parts only, finely chopped

3 large radishes, finely chopped

1 large cucumber, peeled, seeded, and cut into ¼" pieces

1 12-oz. piece boneless beef chuck, trimmed and cut into ⅓" pieces

8 cups kvass or sparkling cider, chilled

¼ cup finely chopped fresh dill

2 hard-cooked eggs, peeled and finely chopped

Dark rye bread, for serving (optional)

SERVES 6-8

1 Bring a 4-qt. saucepan of salted water to a boil and cook carrots just until tender, 3–4 minutes. Drain carrots and let cool, then transfer to a large bowl and set aside. Add potatoes to pan, cover with salted water, and bring to a boil. Reduce heat to medium-low and cook potatoes until tender, about 5 minutes. Drain potatoes and let cool, then transfer to bowl with carrots. Add scallions, radishes, and cucumber to the bowl and cover with plastic wrap. Chill vegetables until ready to use.

2 Add beef to pan and cover with salted water; bring to a boil. Reduce heat to medium-low and cook, covered, until beef is tender, 40–45 minutes. Drain beef and let cool, then transfer to a bowl, cover with plastic wrap, and chill for 30 minutes.

3 Add beef to vegetable mixture. Fold in kvass, dill, eggs, and salt. Serve chilled with rye bread.

Earthy beets, cooked, chilled, and blended with yogurt, dill, and lemon, make for a bright, perfectly balanced borscht-inspired soup. Dill-lemon ice cubes keep this summery concoction cold.

COLD BEET YOGURT SOUP

FOR THE ICE CUBES

3   tbsp. finely chopped fresh dill

1   tbsp. fresh lemon juice

⅛   tsp. kosher salt

FOR THE SOUP

1   lb. beets, boiled or roasted, chilled, and peeled

1¼   cups plain, full-fat yogurt

¼   cup fresh lemon juice

¼   cup packed roughly chopped fresh dill

½   tsp. kosher salt

SERVES 4

1 Make the ice cubes: Combine dill, lemon juice, and salt in a small bowl and divide among 4 cubes of an ice cube tray. Top off with cold water and freeze until solid.

2 Make the soup: Combine beets, yogurt, lemon juice, dill, and salt in a blender and purée until smooth. Pour soup into bowls and top each with a dill-lemon ice cube.

As a refreshing summertime snack or a light evening dessert, this soup is the perfect balance between sweet tropical fruits, tangy citrus, and fresh mint. You can substitute any mix of tropical fruits in the gazpacho-inspired summer recipe, such as banana, guava, and papaya.

TROPICAL FRUIT & MINT SOUP

2   cups sugar

2   sprigs fresh mint,
    plus leaves to garnish

    Pinch kosher salt

1   whole orange, plus ½ cup
    fresh juice

1   tsp. grated lime zest,
    plus 1 tbsp. fresh lime juice

5   strawberries, hulled
    and finely chopped

2   kiwis, peeled and
    finely chopped

1   small mango, peeled,
    pitted, and finely chopped

¼   small pineapple, peeled,
    cored, and finely chopped

    Raspberries, to garnish

SERVES 4

1 Combine sugar and 3 cups water in a 2-qt. saucepan. Bring to a simmer and cook until sugar dissolves, 1–2 minutes. Transfer syrup to a large bowl and add mint sprigs and salt; let cool and then discard mint.

2 Peel orange with a paring knife and working over a bowl, slice between membranes to release orange supremes onto a cutting board. Squeeze juice into bowl and discard spent fruit. Finely chop orange supremes and add to bowl. Stir in additional orange juice, the lime zest and juice, strawberries, kiwis, mango, and pineapple. Cover with plastic wrap and chill for 30 minutes before serving.

3 To serve, divide fruit soup between bowls and garnish with mint leaves and raspberries.

SUPREMING CITRUS

Supreming is a technique used on citrus to remove the membrane and pith, so that only the sweetest, juiciest part of the fruit is reserved.

1 Cut off the ends of the fruit: Using a chef's knife, cut a thin slice from the top and bottom of the fruit to expose the flesh.

2 Cut away the peel and pith: Stand the fruit on a cutting board on a flat end. Following the curve of the fruit, cut away all the peel and white pith. Continue in this fashion, working your way around the fruit.

3 Trim any remaining pith: Trim off any leftover white pith using the tip of the knife.

4 Release the segments: Working over a bowl, make a cut on both sides of each segment to free it from the membrane, letting the segment and juice drop into the bowl below.

When stone fruits are overflowing at the farmers' market, serve this warmly spiced dessert. You can choose whatever looks best: plums, peaches, nectarines, or apricots. Just remember: The riper, the better.

SPICED PLUM SOUP

2½ lb. ripe plums, halved and pitted

2 cups unsweetened apple juice

5 green cardamom pods, lightly crushed

5 whole black peppercorns, lightly crushed

1 stick cinnamon, halved

1 2″ piece ginger, unpeeled and smashed

¼ cup honey

Juice of ½ lemon

Pinch kosher salt

Sour cream, to garnish

SERVES 4-6

1 Combine plums, apple juice, and 1½ cups water in a 6-qt. saucepan. Place cardamom, peppercorns, cinnamon, and ginger on a piece of cheesecloth; tie into a tight bundle and add to pan. Bring to a simmer over medium and cook until plums are tender, about 30 minutes; let cool.

2 Discard spice bundle and transfer mixture to a blender. Add honey, lemon juice, and salt and purée until smooth. If you like, strain soup through a fine-mesh sieve into a bowl. Cover soup with plastic wrap and chill for 1 hour. Ladle soup into bowls and garnish with a swirl of sour cream.

Balsamic vinegar is a natural partner for strawberries; reduced to a syrup-like consistency, it adds a pleasant punch of acidity, bringing out the fruit's natural tartness. Semisweet white wine and woodsy rosemary round out this delectable dessert soup.

STRAWBERRY SOUP WITH BALSAMIC REDUCTION

1   cup semisweet white wine, such as Riesling

1   cup sugar

1   sprig fresh rosemary
    Pinch kosher salt

16   large strawberries, hulled

½   cup balsamic vinegar

SERVES 4

1 Combine wine, sugar, and 1½ cups water in a 2-qt. saucepan. Bring to a simmer and cook until sugar dissolves, 1–2 minutes. Transfer syrup to a blender and add rosemary and salt; let cool and then discard rosemary. Add 14 strawberries and purée until smooth, then strain soup through a fine-mesh sieve into a bowl. Cover with plastic wrap and chill for 1 hour. Slice remaining strawberries and set aside.

2 Meanwhile, heat vinegar in a 1-qt. saucepan over medium and simmer until thickened and syrupy, 8 minutes. Let cool.

3 Ladle soup into chilled glasses or bowls, garnish with sliced strawberries, and drizzle with balsamic reduction.

Sweet-tart blueberries are the foundation for this delicious berry soup, which is flavored with just a trio of ingredients: sugar, lemon, and cinnamon. A mound of whipped cream on each serving adds a touch of richness to this refreshing dessert.

FINNISH BLUEBERRY SOUP

3 pints blueberries

¾ cup sugar

1 stick cinnamon

Grated zest and juice of 1 lemon

2 tbsp. cornstarch, mixed with 2 tbsp. cold water

Pinch kosher salt

Whipped cream, for serving

SERVES 4–6

Bring blueberries and 3 cups water to a boil in a 4-qt. saucepan. Reduce heat to medium and cook, stirring occasionally, until berries begin to burst, about 12 minutes. Strain mixture through a fine-mesh sieve set over a bowl, saving cooking liquid; using a spoon, gently press the berries to extract all their juice, and then discard berries. Return berry soup to saucepan. Add sugar, cinnamon, and lemon zest and juice and bring to a boil. Stir cornstarch mixture into soup and cook until slightly thickened, 3–5 minutes. Discard cinnamon stick and add salt. Ladle soup into bowls and garnish with a dollop of whipped cream.

Canned peaches are a staple of Americana—and are welcome when fresh peaches are not in season. Here, they're combined with cooked carrot and puréed into a delicate dessert soup, which is thickened with Greek yogurt and seasoned with ginger and lime juice.

COLD PEACH SOUP

1 carrot, peeled and thinly sliced

1 ¼″ piece ginger, peeled and thinly sliced

½ cup plain, full-fat Greek yogurt

2 tbsp. half-and-half

2 tsp. fresh lime juice

1 1-qt. jar or can peaches in syrup, drained

Pinch kosher salt

¼ cup sliced almonds, lightly toasted, to garnish

SERVES 4

Simmer carrot, ginger, and 1½ cups water in a 1-qt. saucepan over medium-high until carrot is tender, about 5 minutes. Using a slotted spoon, transfer carrot and ginger to a blender along with ¾ cup cooking liquid; let cool slightly. Add yogurt, half-and-half, lime juice, peaches, and salt, and purée until smooth. Chill for 1 hour before serving. Ladle soup into bowls and garnish with almonds.

THE FUNDAMENTALS: BASIC STOCKS

BEEF STOCK

3   medium yellow onions, halved

12 lb. beef shin bones, cut into 2″ pieces
    (ask your butcher to do this)

3   leeks, trimmed

3   ribs celery, trimmed

2   medium carrots, peeled

1   bouquet garni (page 18)

1   bunch fresh flat-leaf parsley

MAKES ABOUT 4 QUARTS

1 Place onions, cut side down, in a large stockpot.
Cook over high, without turning, until blackened,
5–7 minutes. Transfer onions to a bowl and set aside.

2 Heat pot over high and, working in batches, cook
shin bone pieces, turning as needed, until browned,
15–20 minutes.

3 Reduce heat to medium-high and return all bone pieces
to pot. Stir in reserved onions, the leeks, celery, carrots,
bouquet garni, and parsley and cook, covered, for 20 minutes.
Add 6 qt. water and bring to a boil. Reduce heat to medium
and simmer, uncovered and skimming as needed, for 2½
hours. Pour stock through a fine-mesh sieve set over a bowl,
discarding solids, and let cool. Cover bowl with plastic
wrap and chill until fat rises to the surface and sets. Discard
fat and transfer stock to airtight containers. Refrigerate
for 1 week or freeze for up to 6 months.

BROWN CHICKEN STOCK

5   lb. chicken bones or wings

3   carrots, coarsely chopped

3   ribs celery, coarsely chopped

3   small yellow onions, coarsely chopped

2   tbsp. tomato paste

2   cups dry white wine

10 whole black peppercorns

3   sprigs fresh flat-leaf parsley

2   bay leaves

2   cloves garlic

2   plum tomatoes, coarsely chopped

MAKES ABOUT 3 QUARTS

1 Heat oven to 400°F. Place chicken bones in a large
roasting pan. Roast until golden, 1–1½ hours. Stir in
carrots, celery, onions, and tomato paste and continue
roasting until vegetables and bones are well browned,
about 40 minutes more. Transfer bones and vegetables
to a large stockpot and set aside.

2 Place roasting pan on the stove top over medium-high.
Add wine and bring to a simmer. Deglaze, stirring and
scraping up browned bits from bottom of pan, and transfer
to stockpot. Add peppercorns, parsley, bay leaves, garlic,
tomatoes, and 16 cups water to pot. Bring to a simmer over
medium and cook, skimming as needed, for 3 hours.

3 Pour stock through a fine-mesh sieve set over a bowl,
discarding solids, and let cool. Cover bowl with plastic
wrap and chill until fat rises to the surface and sets. Discard
fat and transfer stock to airtight containers. Refrigerate
for 1 week or freeze for up to 6 months.

PRESSURE COOKER CHICKEN STOCK

3 lb. chicken bones or wings
1/4 tsp. whole black peppercorns
2 carrots, coarsely chopped
1 head garlic, halved crosswise
1 leek, coarsely chopped and rinsed
1 medium yellow onion, quartered

MAKES ABOUT 2 QUARTS

1 Combine all ingredients with 8 cups water in a pressure cooker. Cover pressure cooker with lid and seal according to manufacturer's directions. Heat on high pressure for 5 minutes, then reduce heat to low pressure and cook for 30–40 minutes. (If pressure builds too much and steam escapes rapidly from release valve, remove pot from heat for a few minutes to prevent overpressurizing. Return to low heat when pressure stabilizes.)

2 Remove pressure cooker from heat, but do not remove the lid. The cooling process will decrease pressure naturally, about 20 minutes. This depressurizing also allows the extraction process to continue gently. Once the pot has fully depressurized, remove the lid.

3 Pour stock through a fine-mesh sieve set over a bowl, discarding solids, and let cool. Cover bowl with plastic wrap and chill until fat rises to the surface and sets. Discard fat and transfer stock to airtight containers. Refrigerate for 1 week or freeze for up to 6 months.

CLASSIC DUCK STOCK

2 tsp. kosher salt
8 black peppercorns
1 bay leaf
1 duck carcass, coarsely chopped
1 large yellow onion, quartered
2 cups duck demi-glace

MAKES ABOUT 2½ QUARTS

1 Heat oven to 500°F. Combine salt, peppercorns, bay leaf, duck carcass, and onion in a large roasting pan and roast until deeply browned, about 45 minutes.

2 Remove pan from oven and add 12 cups water. Using a wooden spoon, stir and scrape up any browned bits stuck to bottom of pan, and then return pan to oven. Roast until stock has reduced by half, about 30 minutes.

3 Pour stock through a fine-mesh sieve set over a bowl, discarding solids, and let cool. Cover bowl with plastic wrap and chill until fat rises to the surface and sets. Discard fat and transfer stock to airtight containers. Refrigerate for 1 week or freeze for up to 6 months.

THE SCIENCE OF THE PRESSURE COOKER

When it was first invented, the pressure cooker was called the "digester." This was in the late 16th century, and the inventor, Denis Papin, was a French physicist making the science of the day useful in the kitchen (though he could have used a little help with the branding). Later the machine was called a fast cooker, which was a better name, since one thing a pressure cooker does is speed up steps that often take much longer.

For example, the cooking time for rice drops from 20 or 30 minutes to 6 or 7 minutes. In an hour or two, soup stocks take on the kind of richness they achieve only after bubbling for half a day on the stove top. Bones yield the tough-to-get fats trapped inside in a fraction of the time. Beans can go from tough to tender in as little as 25 minutes (it still helps to soak them before cooking).

So how does it work? Cooking under pressure has two main effects. First, a pressure cooker raises the temperature of steam past the normal boiling point. Inside a sealed pot, temperatures can blaze as high as 250°F. These high temperatures push the natural sugar content of the ingredients inside into caramelization territory, unlocking a different kind of complexity and sweetness in otherwise familiar foods. Second, the higher-pressure environment inside a sealed

cooker can force superheated steam or water deep inside ingredients, so that stew meats can take on that perfectly tender, pull-apart juiciness in the time it takes to watch an episode or two of your favorite television show.

The upshot is that pressure cookers are quick and efficient, yielding terrific results with little intervention.

FISH STOCK

3 lb. fish bones and heads, such as snapper, sole, or halibut, cut into 3″ pieces

2 tbsp. whole black peppercorns

6 sprigs fresh flat-leaf parsley

6 sprigs fresh thyme

2 bay leaves

1 carrot, thinly sliced

1 medium leek, thinly sliced and rinsed

1 medium yellow onion, thinly sliced

1 small bulb fennel, trimmed and thinly sliced

1 cup dry white wine

MAKES ABOUT 1½ QUARTS

Combine fish bones and heads, peppercorns, parsley, thyme, bay leaves, carrot, leek, onion, and fennel in an 8-qt. saucepan. Cook, covered, over medium until vegetables are soft, 12–15 minutes. Add wine and 4 cups cold water and bring to a simmer; cook for 25 minutes. Let stock cool, covered, for 1 hour. Pour stock through a fine-mesh sieve into a bowl, discarding solids, and let cool. Transfer stock to airtight containers. Refrigerate for 1 week or freeze for up to 1 month.

DUNGENESS CRAB STOCK

1 tsp. crushed red chile flakes

1 tsp. dried thyme

8 sprigs fresh flat-leaf parsley

5 whole black peppercorns

2 bay leaves

2 lemons, halved

2 whole live Dungeness crabs

2 tbsp. unsalted butter

2 carrots, coarsely chopped

2 ribs celery, coarsely chopped

1 large yellow onion, coarsely chopped

1 small bulb fennel, trimmed and coarsely chopped

1 cup tomato paste

1 cup brandy

4 sprigs fresh thyme

MAKES ABOUT 1½ QUARTS

1 Combine chile flakes, dried thyme, parsley, peppercorns, bay leaves, lemons, and 16 cups water in an 8-qt. saucepan and bring to a boil. Add crabs and boil until cooked, about 15 minutes. Using tongs, transfer crabs to an ice bath until chilled. Transfer cooking liquid, herbs, and lemons to a bowl and set aside. Clean crabs, reserving crabmeat for soup. Discard top shell, reserving brown meat and tomalley; chop crab leg shells into small pieces.

2 Add butter to pan and melt over medium-high. Add carrots, celery, onion, and fennel and cook until soft, about 15 minutes. Stir in tomato paste and cook for 2 minutes. Add brandy; deglaze, stirring and scraping up browned bits from the bottom of the pan, and cook until reduced by half, 3–4 minutes. Add reserved cooking liquid, brown meat, tomalley, shells, and fresh thyme and bring to a boil. Reduce heat to medium and cook until vegetables are tender and stock is slightly reduced, about 1 hour. Let stock cool slightly and then discard thyme sprigs. Using an immersion blender or regular blender, purée stock until smooth.

3 Pour stock through a fine-mesh sieve set over a bowl, discarding solids, and let cool. Transfer stock to airtight containers. Refrigerate for 1 week or freeze for up to 1 month.

VEGETABLE STOCK

3	tbsp. extra-virgin olive oil
6	cloves garlic, roughly chopped
2	stalks celery, roughly chopped
2	medium onions, roughly chopped
1	bulb fennel, roughly chopped
1	carrot, roughly chopped
1	large leek, roughly chopped and rinsed
1	small tomato, roughly chopped
1	cup dry white wine
6	black peppercorns
5	sprigs fresh flat-leaf parsley
1	bay leaf

MAKES 2 QUARTS

Heat oil in a large pot over medium. Add vegetables and cook until soft, about 15 minutes. Add wine, peppercorns, parsley, bay leaf, and 7 cups water. Bring stock to a boil, skimming off any foam. Lower heat, cover, and simmer for 45 minutes. Pour stock through a fine-mesh sieve set over a bowl and discard solids; let cool. Transfer stock to airtight containers. Refrigerate for 1 week or freeze for up to 1 month.

ROASTED MUSHROOM STOCK

1	lb. white button mushrooms, quartered
5	tbsp. extra-virgin olive oil
2	cloves garlic, smashed
1	carrot, coarsely chopped
1	large yellow onion, coarsely chopped
1	rib celery, coarsely chopped
¼	cup sherry (optional)
½	tsp. whole black peppercorns
6	dried porcini mushrooms
1	bouquet garni (page 18)

MAKES ABOUT 2 QUARTS

1 Heat oven to 450°F. Toss white button mushrooms and 3 tbsp. oil on a baking sheet and roast, stirring occasionally, until golden brown, 15–20 minutes. Set aside.

2 Heat remaining oil in a large stockpot over high. Cook garlic, carrot, onion, and celery until soft, 8–10 minutes. Stir in sherry, peppercorns, porcini, and bouquet garni and cook for 2 minutes. Add reserved white button mushrooms and 10 cups water and simmer until reduced to 8 cups, 30 minutes.

3 Pour stock through a fine-mesh sieve set over a bowl, discarding solids, and let cool. Transfer stock to airtight containers. Refrigerate for 1 week or freeze for up to 6 months.

ICHIBAN DASHI

2	oz. shredded makombu
1¼	cups bonito flakes

MAKES ABOUT 3½ QUARTS

Bring 1 gallon water and makombu to a gentle boil in a 6-qt. saucepan. Using a slotted spoon, remove makombu. (You can save it for another stock, but note that the flavor will not be as pronounced in the second use.) Add bonito flakes. As soon as stock comes to a boil, remove from heat, and pour stock through a fine-mesh sieve set over a bowl, discarding solids; let cool. Transfer stock to airtight containers. Refrigerate for 1 week or freeze for up to 1 month.

INDEX

TABLE OF EQUIVALENTS

The exact equivalents in the following tables have been rounded for convenience.

Liquid and Dry Measurements

U.S.	METRIC
¼ teaspoon	1.25 milliliters
½ teaspoon	2.5 milliliters
1 teaspoon	5 milliliters
1 tablespoon (3 teaspoons)	15 milliliters
1 fluid ounce	30 milliliters
¼ cup	65 milliliters
⅓ cup	80 milliliters
1 cup	235 milliliters
1 pint (2 cups)	480 milliliters
1 quart (4 cups, 32 fluid ounces)	950 milliliters
1 gallon (4 quarts)	3.8 liters
1 ounce (by weight)	28 grams
1 pound	454 grams
2.2 pounds	1 kilogram

Length Measures

U.S.	METRIC
⅛ inch	3 millimeters
¼ inch	6 millimeters
½ inch	12 millimeters
1 inch	2.5 centimeters

Oven Temperatures

FAHRENHEIT	CELSIUS	GAS
250°	120°	½
275°	140°	1
300°	150°	2
325°	160°	3
350°	180°	4
375°	190°	5
400°	200°	6
425°	220°	7
450°	230°	8
475°	240°	9
500°	260°	10

ACKNOWLEDGMENTS

Many people deserve recognition for their contributions to the making of this cookbook. Chief among them are SAVEUR former food editor Kellie Evans, who curated existing recipes and developed new ones, and SAVEUR test kitchen director Farideh Sadeghin, who tested recipes, prepared dishes for photography, and generally helped bring this volume to fruition. Thanks also to test kitchen assistant Jake Cohen—not to mention the many former kitchen staff members and chefs whose recipes made the final cut of our favorite soups and stews. On the writing and editing side, thanks go to deputy editor Yaran Noti, senior editors Sophie Brickman and Mari Uyehara, assistant editor Alexander Testere, and a group of writers and interns, including Genevieve Ko, Teri Tsang Barrett, Laura Grahame, and Giancarlo Buonomo. For the visuals in the book, we especially thank SAVEUR photo editor Michelle Heimerman, staff photographer Matt Taylor-Gross, photographer Joseph DeLeo, and stylist Judy Haubert, along with the many others whose work is represented here. And finally, a special thanks to managing editor Camille Rankin, whose oversight of this project helped us all get to the gate on time.

On the publishing side, we are extremely grateful to our partners at Weldon Owen for their vision and expert handling of this latest book in our ongoing collaboration. Thanks go in particular to Kelly Booth and her colleague Marisa Kwek for the beautiful design of the book; to Terry Newell, Amy Kaneko, and Roger Shaw for bringing it to the consumer; and, most of all, to Amy Marr, associate publisher, for her leadership and unflagging optimism during the inevitable ups and downs of bringing this project to completion.

—Adam Sachs

PHOTOGRAPHY CREDITS

Cover photograph by Marcus Nilsson and food styling by Victoria Granof

Andre Baranowski 51; **Elizabeth Cecil** 7, 11; **Todd Coleman** 6, 17, 23, 26, 34, 60, 94, 98, 152, 179, 185, 186; **Joseph De Leo** 1, 2, 14, 29, 37, 38, 48, 54, 57, 63, 64, 68, 71, 82, 93, 103, 106, 115, 122, 134, 138, 159, 163, 168, 182, 201, 204, 208; **Penny De Los Santos** 128; **Dylan + Jeni** 41; **Chris Granger** 44; **Michelle Heimerman** 80-81, 126-127, 212-213; **Ingalls Photography** 72, 85, 86, 143, 144, 176; **Ray Kachatorian** 156; **John Lee** 12-13, 42-43, 66-67, 104-105, 132-133, 166-167, 192-193; **Landon Nordeman** 77; **James Oseland** 20; **Bill Phelps** 137; **Vanessa Rees** 118; **Farideh Sadeghin** 171; **Shutterstock** 90, 125, 175; **Matt Taylor-Gross** 8, 10, 33, 47, 97, 109, 110, 121, 151, 160, 197, 207; **Romulo Yanes** 191, 194, 198

SAVEUR SOUPS AND STEWS

Editor-in-Chief **Adam Sachs**
Deputy Editor **Yaran Noti**
Managing Editor **Camille Rankin**

Weldon Owen Inc.

Associate Publisher **Amy Marr**
Creative Director **Kelly Booth**
Art Director **Marisa Kwek**

Weldon Owen wishes to thank Amanda Anselmino,
Ethel Brennan, Georgeanne Brennan, Sarah Putman
Clegg, Gloria Geller, Lillian Kang, Stephen Lam,
John Lee, Monica Lee, Rachel Markowitz, Caroline
Miller, Sharon Silva, Elizabeth Parson, and Emma
Rudolph for their help producing this book.

Conceived and produced with SAVEUR
by Weldon Owen Inc., 1045 Sansome Street,
San Francisco, California 94111
www.weldonowen.com

ISBN-13: 978-1-61628-965-2
ISBN-10: 1-61628-965-1

Printed in China by RR Donnelley

Library of Congress Cataloging in Publication
data is available.

First edition
10 9 8 7 6 5 4 3 2 1